RECHARGE YOUR LIBRARY PROGRAMS WITH POP CULTURE AND TECHNOLOGY

Connect with Today's Teens

Linda D. Behen

LIBRARIES UNLIMITED

AN IMPRINT OF ABC-CLIO, LLC
Santa Barbara, California • Denver, Colorado • Oxford, England

Copyright 2013 by ABC-CLIO, LLC

Library of Congress Cataloging-in-Publication Data

Behen, Linda D.
   Recharge your library programs with pop culture and technology : connect with today's teens /
Linda D. Behen.
      pages cm
   Includes bibliographical references and index.
   ISBN 978–1–61069–369–1 (hard copy) — ISBN 978–1–61069–370–7 (ebook) 1. Libraries and
teenagers—United States. 2. High school libraries—Activity programs—United States. 3. Young adults'
libraries—Activity programs—United States. 4. High school libraries—Information technology—United
States. 5. Young adults' libraries—Information technology—United States. I. Title.
Z718.5B44   2013
025.5′678223—dc23   2013007683

ISBN: 978–1–61069–369–1
EISBN: 978–1–61069–370–7

17 16 15 14 13   1 2 3 4 5

This book is also available on the World Wide Web as an eBook.
Visit www.abc-clio.com for details.

Libraries Unlimited
An Imprint of ABC-CLIO, LLC

ABC-CLIO, LLC
130 Cremona Drive, P.O. Box 1911
Santa Barbara, California 93116-1911

This book is printed on acid-free paper ∞

Manufactured in the United States of America

Contents

Preface: Why We Do What We Do

I believe that today and tomorrow are the best times to be a librarian, especially a librarian that works with teens. Keeping up with technology changes, pop culture, and the average student's "minute to get it" attention span is likely to be the most personally and professionally enriching time of our careers. We can't do what librarians did in the past; we can't spend a majority of our time tending to our collections and shelves. We can't use stale instruction methods to teach information literacy; in fact, we can't focus only on information. We need to use every service, every encounter, and every instructional opportunity to integrate media literacy into students' academic and personal lives. And we need to connect with them through what they find interesting and relevant.

Perks of being school librarians in today's world include having a great excuse for being an early adopter of tech gadgets, reading *People* magazine, watching *Dancing with the Stars*, reading the *Hunger Games* trilogy without apology, and discovering and using all the creative and well designed media tools and apps to share with our communities.

No matter how we shun and look down on pop culture and academic entertainment, it is a factor, method, and tool to engage and connect with today's students. Video, messaging and texting, gaming, and television are the hooks to pull students deep into the subject content of school curriculum. Is using pop culture and technology trends to recharge our library program any less serious and intellectual than using scavenger hunts to discover the location of the library's encyclopedias, almanacs, and dictionaries, or presenting booktalks when students can read the inside covers of books themselves?

We have always done just about anything, short of standing on our heads, to help students learn about the invaluable library resources, services, and tools that are their lifeline to successful academic experiences, and rich, full lives. As librarians, we know that life's tools and secrets lie in libraries, and that an individual's ability to think critically, consider and find solutions to problems, and ask for help when necessary are all the tools and methods needed for information literacy and making it out in the big world.

Congratulate yourself on becoming and continuing to serve as a librarian who interacts daily with teens and preteens. We have at least 180 days a year to make a difference in our students' lives. We have so much to share and a zillion ways to share it. Find your best approach and style, and go out and reinvent your library program for today's generation.

If any of the ideas and methods in this book inspire one, two, or three other school librarians to experiment, create, or try something new and different, I will feel as though the time spent writing this book has been well worth it. Go now, and design your new image; become your avatar or the superhero of your dreams.

1

Schools and Libraries in Transition: So Much More Than Materials, Reference, and a Reading Room

It's the universal chicken and the egg dilemma: Did patrons' changing needs and desires come first, or did librarians' vision of patrons' wants and needs begin the transition to today's libraries? If you know the answer, please raise your hand.

One thing we all know is that libraries are undergoing huge changes. Libraries are no longer warehouses of information where a patron arrives, selects, and reads the information at home or in a quiet library space. In fact, patrons don't need to "arrive" at our facility at all, and they are able to interact with information that we provide without ever speaking to a librarian or staff member. And the methods of interaction have expanded to include reading print materials from an iPad or other desktop, laptop, or tablet screen; listening to the material with an MP3, smart phone, or iPod Touch; or playing with information through game formats or videos. Links are often included within text so that we can jump away from the material itself to investigate a related topic. I've, more than once, traveled such links down far and winding paths never to return to the origin or topic where I began. In addition, our relationship with information has expanded beyond reading, thinking, and assimilating to include adaptation, curation, and conversion of data and information into all types of results. Students, teachers, staff, and administrators are taking information that they locate in endless ways, and assembling it into videos, audio, graphic documents, and other presentation formats. The expectation for today's libraries is to provide the information and tools needed for our users to find, access, and create.

Library resources, and access to those resources, now include social media. Teen and adult librarians blog and tweet for and with their patrons about books, services, and programs, and the information shared among individuals through social networks is valued.

A simple Google search of the terms "public library" and "Skype" results in over 2 million hits, including learning how to Skype, reasons to Skype with your friends and family, keeping military families connected, and learning about the power of Skype. Consider how many results there would be if you included all types of libraries and educational institutions; for several years, teachers and school librarians have been using Facetime and Skype to connect with authors and experts. My day (personal and professional) isn't complete until I catch up with my favorite blogs and tweets, and many ideas that I've introduced to my school and community began with 140 characters from Twitter.

This inclusion of social media is a hugely transformative adoption. It suddenly appears that librarians, scholars and experts, institutions of higher learning, museums, and schools have agreed that there is value in what ordinary people know and share. Wikipedia has led the way and demonstrated the benefit of crowd sourcing to share expertise and knowledge. Google and Wikipedia searchers have learned the value of reliability and credibility through the open editing problems we all witnessed in the early days of Wikipedia. Social media has become simply another source of information added to the traditional sources like encyclopedia and reference materials, journal, magazine, and newspaper articles, and websites that students must learn to search, select and evaluate. And it's a format that students and others can now, and in the future, use to share their own personal knowledge and expertise.

Over the past few years, I've been witness to a significant increase of cooperation among types of libraries. School libraries are encouraged by local public and academic libraries to borrow materials for students. I am giddy when I request books, music, and journal articles electronically from university and public libraries with hardly an interruption in my day. I can audition these books and materials with our patrons before investing in permanent purchases, or I can choose to continue to rely on my ILL friends in other libraries for the books that I use just once a year. In return, I constantly spread awareness of these good-willed interlibrary loans, and the institutions, to students and teachers; I shout these golden library opportunities far and wide. Satisfied students who are happy with the items they have been loaned are encouraged to continue requesting help and materials from other libraries. Transactions like these do more than provide needed information. They are forms of information literacy that are essential; students' familiarity with approaching and accessing other libraries (usually larger) makes them more confident and is likely to ease the transition to higher academic libraries.

Never have we, and our patrons, had so many choices. Library users, and especially students, are interacting differently with information in today's world. They access the information that we make available in a seemingly endless variety of ways, they learn how to evaluate that information and assimilate it, they figure out why citations and bibliographies are important to the academic world, and they build their projects and assignments using many new and exciting formats and media. Reference questions are asked 24/7 through e-mail, texts, tweets, messaging, and in person; the only barrier to asking for information is self-imposed limits.

Reading rooms of the past are being reinvented, and they now serve many purposes. Libraries in transition still have quiet reading areas with soft seating, but we also have moveable tables and group areas so that users can spread out and study or work in groups. Libraries leading the change provide smart boards, monitors, cameras, and more to accommodate students' wishes and needs, and the spaces aren't so quiet anymore. In addition, devices such as laptops and book readers are loaned to students who don't have their own and who wish to take them home.

A trend moving through universities is the Learning Commons (LC). The LC is a bustling and open area intended for constant interaction among students, instructors, librarians, and combinations of people and groups. The LC is frequently part of, or designed in collaboration with, the library. As with other trends that begin at universities, school libraries are starting to model their school learning resource centers or libraries after the LC. Today's school libraries come with many different names; library, media center, library–media center, information center, learning center, and learning commons are used to describe a school space with resources and tools. But no matter what the name and what the essential resources and space are comprised of, it seems that we all share a common mission of providing all possible methods of information, learning, and help. School libraries are currently in an expansion mode as we attempt to broaden our collections and services to include all things in all formats for all needs and all patrons.

My public library, the Public Library of Cincinnati and Hamilton County (PLCH), has changed tremendously in the last decade, and I've noticed even more rapid change in the past year or two. I wouldn't trade my iPad or iPhone PLCH app for a first edition *Pride and Prejudice*. Really. It only takes me seconds to renew or place a hold on a title through the app. Luckily, my public library still holds and provides easy access to scholarly and research-intended information, but PLCH has recently redesigned its space to include the Popular Library, which provides the obvious popular materials, formats, and information on the easily accessible ground floor. Technology serves useful purposes— the self-checkout makes the loan experience fast, usually simple, and very private. In addition, in urban settings, public libraries seem to be fulfilling an unintended social service along with all of their other services—many individuals who have nowhere else to spend a frigid or hot day can find refuge in the library. I can imagine a future in which a social services agency will staff an office in the public library in order to meet with its clients in the space where they are likely to be.

Academic libraries, along with school libraries, have more complicated tasks and missions. I like to think of an academic library as a school library's older sibling that takes care of and educates the students that we prepare for them. Both academic and school libraries are part of a larger organization, and those universities, colleges, and schools often determine how and at what speed their libraries change. Our academic and school libraries exist to help fulfill our institution's mission and objectives, and, in most cases, we don't have complete autonomy to define our role, methods, and identity. On the other hand, the relationship is mutually satisfying. We benefit from working with subject experts, teachers, and professors who often bring new and exciting information and tools to us and enlighten our lives. We are provided a budget or handfuls of money to create our collections and programs. We enjoy getting to know students through extracurricular activities and by attending student performances, and we teach to a somewhat captive audience. I always feel that I am first a teacher in my professional role; nothing is more satisfying than watching and participating in students' intellectual growth and maturity throughout the years that they spend with us.

I, for one, would not want to go back to the so-called simple days of print collections, reference, and silent reading rooms. Who doesn't thank the universe and those really smart guys like Steve Jobs, Bill Gates, and Mark Zuckerberg for the ease and entertainment we enjoy through technology? I'd like to personally kneel before the individuals who created searchable databases and keyword searching. What fraction of time do we now spend searching eBooks or journal articles for a subject, topic, or keyword in contrast with yesterday's searching within print collections by *The Reader's Guide*, book index, table of contents, or page by page?

We thought the databases, eBooks, and digital book readers of the 1990s and early 2000s were game changers, but those tools were electronic tools used in a traditional way. Most—if not all—digital books, supplemental textbook information, and research articles were duplications of the print material. Students accessed, searched, read, assimilated, evaluated, re-searched, and so on and so on. It was still an era of black and white print, even if the computer screen was the mode of access. In addition to using computers, students and teachers frequently (very frequently) printed off copies to read more easily and to use as backup of a rarely trusted machine. Little—if anything—was interactive, there was no cloud computing, and there weren't many options beyond writing research papers and using PowerPoint to complete assignments and projects.

Today's learners eagerly push technological boundaries in the classroom. Students create videos and edit them like pros. Their presentations include Prezi, original images and digitally enhanced photos, YouTube videos, segments of streaming videos from databases, and audio soundtracks. The large files are saved easily and dependably to the cloud in Dropbox or Google Drive, and teachers no longer worry how students will access their files to present to the class.

We know that these digital natives don't have the fear or dread of technology that we tech immigrants have. And as digital natives, they assume that they understand all things digital and tech. But we see them struggle to find information that is reliable, appropriate, accurate, and current, and their teachers constantly let us know that students are settling for easy, shallow information and research methods. It seems that almost daily I hear teachers talk about how students don't understand technology and digital information to the extent that they think, and they have difficulty using any kind of information beyond their personal social needs.

Is it a huge problem that digital natives don't come to us with the foundation we are expecting and sophisticated knowledge of information, media, and technology literacy? Is finding only easy and shallow information a generational problem? Is a three-second attention span and desire to seek easy information a sign of this generation's intellectual demise? And are these issues new? I don't think they are new, and our students—teens, preteens, pre-preteens—have always been resistant to what they are forced to learn in the classroom and to what isn't fun. Why else would the government, psychologists, and educational professionals discuss adaptations and spend so much money trying out new and improved methods in order to reach every child, recognize individual learning styles, find success with the Socratic method, change the entire school's structure in order to accommodate the block schedule, focus on the common core, and hope that no child is left behind? What is new and exciting and able to solve the "minute to get it" attention span and attitude, is that we have so many tools and methods available for teaching fundamentals, deep reading, and critical thinking through classroom curriculum and school libraries.

The ability that this generation demonstrates with phones, computers, and gaming devices provides the tech agility and fertile environment for the knowledge that educators can provide to ensure depth of knowledge. And it makes our role as school librarians exciting. We get to find the good stuff and use methods to teach that get students excited. School librarians have always been the scouts and discoverers of the best tools and practices of information searching, gathering, and using. We can now corral our eager, tech-agile students and teach them how to be successful in their academic pursuits and, ultimately, to become curious and ever seeking lifelong learners.

Teachers are as bored with the same text-heavy presentation tools and presentations as students are. Three teachers, without prompting from me this year, have pleaded with me to teach students about newer and better tools for presentation projects. And now, students and teachers are coming to the library to learn not only about information, research, and assimilation, but also about the newest methods of assessment and to show off what they know. I might not look forward to teaching multiple classes in the same day about Boolean operators, MLA format, and truncation punctuation, but I do jump up and down with excitement when I see a student's visually attractive media presentation with all of those elements obviously learned and used.

Who would have thought even five years ago that the iPad would be providing us with the latest news about raging fires in the southwest, unrest in the Middle East, and our favorite celebrities; our daily dose of comics; streaming movies and TV shows; tools for school and work; and classic as well as current best-selling novels? And that doesn't begin to cover the available topics and uses of an iPad. As our school finishes the first year of an iPad program that provides all freshmen with their own devices, the daily list of apps that teachers are requesting for their classes is growing more quickly than we ever imagined it would. And as the school librarian, I've added many of my must-haves to the list, including database and information readers, public library apps, the Prezi viewer, dictionaries, and book readers. My absolute favorite app is currently our own library catalog app that allows students and teachers to search our library catalog on the go from any mobile or smart device and that prompts patrons to place holds and check their accounts. It seems that it just can't get any better than having our library in every teacher's and student's backpack, briefcase, pocket, or bag.

How do libraries and educators plan for these rapidly changing times? How do we stop spending our time, money, and energy on what defined us as libraries and librarians in the past, and begin focusing on today's learners' needs, interests, and styles? If we don't adapt and evolve, we are no longer relevant or useful. We all know what happens to those who are no longer relevant or useful—see the "Dinosaur" entry at Wikipedia, http://en.wikipedia.org/wiki/Dinosaur.

Libraries are not dying; they are changing. We've been hearing about the looming demise of libraries since the Internet went public decades ago. Today's global information is available instantly with Google, Wikipedia, and the iPhone's Siri. We also know that our students, teachers, and communities need more than the information that can be retrieved through these sources. The trick is for us to convince our patrons that they need more than search engines, websites, and intelligent personal assistants—it's not possible for our students and patrons to know what they don't know.

Our patrons' quests are becoming more complicated all the time. I've heard the search for information being compared to trying to take a sip from a fire hose. Not only do researchers have information choices from endless sources, they now need to choose among constantly changing formats and devices.

Complicating the issue further, in school and university settings, students need to be assessed. Students are moving quickly beyond PowerPoint and Word documents to wow their teachers and classmates with more dynamic Prezi, Knovio, and Animoto presentations, and their teachers are thrilled to have projects to grade, read, and watch that are as varied and interesting as the students who create them.

With all of these changes, needs, opportunities, frustrations, and stress, we are creating our niche and the necessity for school librarians. We have always been, and need to continue to be, change agents who recommend, teach, advise, and help teachers, students, and administrators. The playing field is larger, our role is larger, and this is our era to lead. It's time to begin the evolution and revolution.

2

Lead the Change

CHANGE IS HARD

"I am not now that which I have been" (George Byron, 1788–1824). This quote by Lord Byron could very well be describing the institution of the library. We are not the library of the 1800s, 1900s, or even the 2000s; and the years between 2000 and 2013 have exploded with challenges, changes, and opportunities. As newer and better methods of research, publishing, and access evolve on a daily if not hourly basis, our libraries, and we, are not what we were yesterday.

Change makes us squirm and furrow our brows. We rightfully argue that we need to be part of the discussion that determines and brings about change in our schools and libraries. We join committees and groups to discuss, encourage, and decide, and still, we feel uncertain and worried when change is imminent.

We long for the simple days when we knew what we knew and what we could expect. We fear failure and cling to our best practices of the past. We have suspicions about early technology adopters, and we wonder if they truly enjoy the newest innovation and progression. We secretly hope that they are just better pretenders than us.

DIGITAL NATIVES VS. TECH IMMIGRANTS

Many of us are tech immigrants whose library school education consisted of print *Reader's Guide to Periodical Literature, Sears List of Subject Headings,* and *Encyclopaedia Britannica.* If we were lucky enough to acquire our library school degree or certification in the 1990s or later, we did gain some computer and Internet experience and knowledge, searched a few dial-up databases by a very structured and controlled vocabulary, or browsed the library's Gopher Protocol network to enjoy a menu-based hierarchy of subjects and documents.

I don't know about you, but those memories make me grateful for today's world of digital reference, copy cataloging, online databases, and online ordering. Not to mention blogs, tweets, webinars and videos that inform me and show me—in the privacy of my own computer device—what I need to know.

The very newest librarians are lucky to begin their careers with the tools that are part of today's pop culture and trends; however, these tools will evolve into something else or be stepped over for the next latest and greatest developments. Even the most and best prepared will become the anxious adapters of tomorrow's technology; we all must travel the tech journey, keep up, and adopt constant change.

ACTIVE DECISION MAKING

Our professional learning and education, as much or more than in other professions, never ends or becomes complete; change is both inevitable and hard. There are changes that we can control and changes that we cannot control. Although the "cannot controls" might be frustrating because they happen around us and we often have no choice, we must always remember that we do have a choice in how we deal with them. The "can controls" are often what give us the most hesitation and heartburn; these opportunities can result in personal failure and error. We don't want to fail and don't want to make mistakes, so we hesitate and take a wait and see approach until the path become clear.

This hesitation is a decision. And it's a decision that makes it harder to move later. The things you ignore seem to pile up with the addition of more information, complications, and newer trends. Consider the decision to purchase and make eBooks and eBook readers available to your patrons. You question if students can be trusted with expensive equipment, if an eBook is a format that you want to promote, and if you want to purchase eBooks from publishers who are making the licensing agreements very difficult for libraries to manage. You might also know how complicated the path to eBooks and eBook readers is, and maybe you are resisting the amount of work involved in determining what you need and want. On the other hand, imagine what you will learn along the path in forming your decision to purchase or not purchase eBooks and eBook readers—you will know of the various electronic book and reader options and be able compare and contrast them for teachers and your principal, you will know what publishers provide what types of materials, you will learn about licensing and copyright issues specific to eBooks, and you might get to know eBook experts in the profession that you can rely on for information and advancements regarding digital materials. In the end, your decision might be to pilot one or two readers, or you might make the decision to use eBooks by purchasing digital titles for Nooks, iPads, or Kindles that your students already own. Any action and effort that you've taken to become informed will be beneficial and is to be commended. Instead of waiting for inspiration and an epiphany, you take action; you gain clarity in your strategy with regard to personal devices and book readers, and you can debate with the best on the pros and cons of the issue. And most importantly, your students and patrons benefit from the addition of any eBooks that you provide. There is no correct answer or method for any library or librarian as long as the decisions are based on the active pursuit of decision making.

Let's take a close look at things that we may or may not be able to control and that might stand in our way of moving forward and creating the best library we can.

OUTSIDE OUR CONTROL

Technology, our school environment, and time are areas that have the most impact on our lives within a school and are likely to be areas in which we have the least amount of control.

Our superintendents, principals, academic deans, and other administrators make decisions daily that affect our programs and professional lives. Sometimes we have opportunities to weigh in and help make the decisions, and sometimes we don't. Being told to adapt and incorporate specific philosophies or tools isn't something that most mere humans find motivating.

Let's look at the areas in our professional lives over which we have the least control—technology, school environment, and time.

Technology

Technology and tools that your school uses and provides, along with the demands on faculty and staff to learn, support, and integrate into today's learners' school life, aren't always the choices that you want or hope to have and use. You may love Apple products, but your school is a PC environment. You may love smart boards, but you have only a digital projector and laptop. You want to connect to patrons through Pinterest and Facebook, but those sites are blocked at school. You may want to migrate to your state's library management system, but your school isn't willing to spend the time and money to make it happen now.

Our schools and school libraries are a microcosm of life; sometimes we just don't have the stuff we want when we want it.

Despite budget woes and restrictions imposed within our schools, technological advances are occurring with or without us, and the transitional period we are in requires schools and libraries to support many formats and technologies. Most of us are streaming video from subscription databases, but we also use our collections of VHS and DVD videos. We have smart boards—and white boards and black boards. We have desktop computers, kiosks and Online Public Access Catalogs (OPACs), and, one-to-one laptop programs; classroom laptop sets in carts; or bring your own device (BYOD) programs. We have iPads and iPod Touches, Kindles, Nooks, and other handheld devices, and, print textbooks and monographs, digital iBooks and eBooks. We have databases full of reference material, newspapers, journals, magazines, images, and primary sources, but we still subscribe to print newspapers, journals, and magazines.

The specific combination of these information sources is unique to each library, but it's unlikely that these duplications of materials will change much in the near future. It may be necessary and useful to have multiple formats and choices for every user's preference and choice, and for each unique situation. These duplications are not surprising when you consider that we've been adding information devices for longer than I can remember; for example, we continue to use radios despite televisions in every home, we still go to movies even though we stream or rent them through Netflix, Hulu, or Red Box. We listen to our music on CDs as well as through iTunes and Pandora, and most homes still have landline phones even though we all carry cell phones.

Your budget is more likely to be shrinking instead of growing, and you wonder how you can afford to keep adding formats and materials without subtracting. You worry that you still haven't figured out the best blogs to follow, but now you feel pushed to embrace Twitter or Pinterest. You've finally created pathfinders on your website with selected websites, databases, and citation tools, but your colleague from another school or building is suggesting that LibGuides is the best tool to use. Today your principal strongly suggests that you attend a summer technology workshop, but last night you booked your vacation for the same week. These times are not simple, but there is no turning back.

School Environments

The school environment is another area outside our control that complicates our professional lives on a daily basis. The school day, calendar, schedule, teaching philosophies and methods, and personalities and attitudes of administrators, teachers, and students are not things that we can adjust to fit our personal needs. Every teacher practices a different style of teaching, and every teacher expects a different relationship with the library and librarian based either on preference or past experiences. Students, teachers, and administration are multitasking like crazy, and students' attention spans and attitudes have been reduced to "a minute to get it." We worry about students' reluctance to think critically and deeply. Debate is ongoing among educators about what and how to teach: do we prepare students best for their adult work lives by focusing more on the lifelong skills of communication, teamwork, and tenacity, or do we want and expect our students to live fuller and richer lives with the ability to recall lines of *King Lear* and the Emancipation Proclamation. And our own job descriptions, responsibilities, and expectations are all areas that can change, with or without our input, as quickly as technology.

As librarians who work in schools and educational institutions that are part of larger faculties and educational institutions, we spend hours and days in meetings and in-services to discuss and broaden our scope of reaching students through differentiated learning, connected learning, play learning, or peer learning, and we debate advantages of one-to-one or bring your own device (BYOD) environments. We are part of the discussion about our faculty and staff's need to communicate better, and commitment to embrace teamwork and collaboration. All these dynamic and continual discussions are invaluable to us as educators, but we still have technology tools to discover and learn about, programming and instruction to create, books to shelve, displays to make, and reports to complete—all amid the constant interruptions and interaction with students and teachers.

Time

Time is a constraint that can be both self-imposed and imposed by others. Time is a great excuse many of us use for saying no or putting off the things we don't want to do. And our excuses, instead of relieving us and providing more time, just keep our to-do list growing and growing. And, managing time —or time management—is that elusive skill that we try to teach our students despite our own struggles with it.

See if some of the following five scenarios that make us feel out of control feel familiar to you:

1. You moved from a block schedule school with 90-minute classes to a traditional eight-bell schedule with 45-minute classes. You've scheduled a class in the library for instruction on Shakespeare's comedies, and the teacher can't give up more than 20 minutes of the class period for your library instruction. You have a powerful game that incorporates information literacy that students loved last year, but now you have to shorten it by more than half and leave out elements that you know are essential.
2. You have been asked to add to your current committees, councils, and student clubs by moderating both the student book club, and the sophomore class, and you haven't even cataloged and processed the 50 books that you ordered in August before school started.
3. The head of the History Department refuses to give up any class time for research instruction because he can more efficiently teach all the tricks and methods he learned when he was in graduate school 15 years ago. The

student questions that come to you in the library indicate that his instruction is not successful.

4. Your library field trip with 20 senior honor students to the state university's library to talk with academic librarians and be guided through the beginning stages of their senior English research paper was cancelled due to a snow day, and there are no more possible days to reschedule.

5. A student who was absent the day of your presentation comes to you for help with his alternative energy research project. You sit down with him, spend 40 minutes walking him through the research guide (pointing out the best databases and information), do a sample search using his specific topic, and show him how to take one of the articles and create a citation for his bibliography using an online bibliography builder. When you're finished, he says, "Do you know of an energy website that I can use instead? I prefer websites because they're easier and I don't need usernames and passwords."

Hopefully, you haven't experienced all of the preceding situations, or at least not in the same week, but trying to balance our goals, time, personalities, and changing environments can be stressful, and your days are likely to be peppered with a variety of inconveniences and barriers beyond your control.

Need more convincing? It is time that I call in a superhero to help you believe that it is time to reinvent your library, yourself, and your career. Let R. David Lankes, professor and Dean's Scholar for the New Librarianship at Syracuse University's School of Information Studies and director of the Information Institute of Syracuse, provide his stellar advice in far more convincing terms than I can. Here is his August 1, 2012, post, "Beyond the Bullet Points: It Is Time to Stop Trying to Save Libraries:"

Close the crisis center. Take down the picket signs. Please proceed to un-occupy the library. It is time to stop trying to save libraries.

No, this is not another bait and switch act of verbal irony about how libraries are obsolete. This is about the messages we send. I became aware of this recently when two colleagues I respect greatly and I were talking about the employment in libraries and the economic downturn. We quickly started talking about opportunities for librarians outside of libraries (an idea I support regardless of the employment in libraries). It wasn't until I thought about it afterwards that I realized this was akin to talking about getting as many passengers off the sinking ship as possible. Where did they get the idea that libraries are sinking? These are smart folks, and not prone to the sky is falling "libraries are relics" rhetoric. Then, to my horror, I realized it was me! I set the premise for the whole conversation. I was the one that felt libraries are so important and librarians so crucial that we must save them. To save anything assumes that they need intervention and are at dire risk of being lost. This messaging is insidious. For example a few years ago I started adding these lines to the beginnings of my presentations: "Best Days of Librarianship are Ahead of Us. We are the Right Profession, Uniquely Positioned to Lead in the Knowledge Age. However, we won't get there following current trends and with our current focus on 'Recorded Knowledge' and Buildings."

It looks initially as a nice little uplifting piece of fluff, but it is really an implied threat. If you continue down this path there will be no bright futures … listen to me so I can save you. The minute that we talk about libraries in the context of threats we reinforce the premise that libraries are in crisis and heading into the sepia color of memory.

We must take on Google (or be like Google, or build our own Google) to save libraries! We must be on Facebook (Twitter, Tumblr, Pinterest) to save libraries!

Screw that!

To be sure libraries need more funding, they need modernization, they need a shifted identity in the minds of our communities. To be sure there are some libraries that need to be saved in the most literal sense from closure, but the whole profession? By taking on the mantra of saving libraries, we are assuming that we are weak. Worse, it plays into the whole idea that we are wounded or broken. I have spent the better part of the last two years talking about advocacy within our communities and stressing that we must give up a deficit model and embrace the aspirations of the community. Rather than talking about how the community can't read, or research, or access the Internet, we need to talk about how reading, researching, or accessing the Internet can help our communities unleash their potential. We should be asking how libraries help our communities thrive. If we can put together that vision in a compelling way, people will support libraries out of self-interest, not out of pity, charity, or a sense of obligation.

Find a thriving library. They are not thriving because they are the best at running around yelling the sky is falling. Playing the role of the poor little library is not endearing, it is, frankly, embarrassing. Even when there is a financial crisis, or even when the community has a crisis of confidence, we should ask for support based on a track record of service and support. Run on your record not the promise to do better (or worse more of the same) in the future.

Now, as you know I define the library as a platform of a librarian—a platform for community learning and innovation. That means that the problem here is not the library, it is us—librarians. I have, for example, played the crisis in libraries card. I have played the libraries are like broccoli and good for you card. I have played on fears as much as aspirations in my time. Worse, I have sat back and let others in and outside of the field do it. I must be the first one to change. I do so humbly pledge to do so. You're next.

First call me on it if I fall back into the "save libraries" narrative, and then pledge to reject it yourself. Let us also to pledge that "Hi, I'm a librarian," doesn't sound like an introduction to a 12 step meeting, but instead rings like a declaration of pride akin to "I'm the Goddamn Batman!"

I believe the future of libraries is bright. I believe that libraries improve society. I believe that libraries are key to positive social transformation. I believe that librarians are facilitators of knowledge. I believe that librarians are the most important assets of any library. It is in my demonstration of these beliefs that I help ensure the future of libraries and librarians. I don't need to save libraries.

Libraries have survived for over 3,000 years. Libraries have survived famine, plagues, prejudice, censorship, and anti-intellectualism well before either of us came along. I don't need to save libraries; I need to help transform them. The test of that transformation is not in a building, or a collection, or a service or even the librarians; it is in the achievements of the community.

Allow Lankes's confidence to fill you with certainty that today is the time to begin recharging, transforming, and redesigning your library program. Become Batman, an avatar, or the superhero of your choice, and do the hard work so that our current and future patrons will experience the best possible community learning and innovation through your library program.

Forge ahead, and take a look at the suggestions and methods in the next chapters that will make your role and job more efficient, successful, and rewarding. Adapt what is offered to fit your students' and school's needs, and spend time wondering how you can provide the best services and instruction beginning right now.

3

Things We Can Control

TIME IS OF THE ESSENCE

Now is the time to reassess what's important to your library program and patrons. It will give you control over what you might perceive as having no control over and will help you in the transition to an evolving library and program.

Reprioritize according to changing library services, programming, interests, and needs. Don't continue to do the same things just because it's always been done that way, or because your students 10 or five years ago really enjoyed it. Keep things fresh and new. Serve today's students with an eye toward tomorrow's learners.

Question constantly what you do. Is it time to stop offering, or to redesign, the reading contests that few participate in? Are you updating your instruction every time you provide research instruction, or are you doing the same things the same way you did last year, or five or more years ago? Do you spend endless hours cataloging and processing books that never circulate? Do you worry endlessly about well-organized shelves and beautiful rows of books? Are you pulling collections of books for classes to browse, only to reshelve them? Are you spending weeks on inventory every spring?

Unless you are part of a system that prevents you from creating your own policies regarding inventory, processing, and circulation, consider these time saving changes. If you are part of a system that does require the continuation of practices that are outdated or unnecessary timestealers, start asking about, suggesting, or debating ways of doing things differently. The following sections present the timesavers.

COLLECTION INVENTORY AND MAINTENANCE

Inventory your collection every other year. A 9- or 10-month period does not warrant a complete inventory. You will lose books—count on it. You will know which popular books are missing because the demand will be your alarm. Replace those books, hope the missing books return so that you will have additional copies, and move on with your other responsibilities. Stand by with boxes when students clean out lockers at the end of the year. Most books are recovered and returned at the end of the year when parents find them under beds, in backpacks, or in the trunks of cars.

A two-year cycle of inventory is plenty to keep your database up-to-date and will allow students to search the catalog and shelves successfully on their own.

Don't Cover Paperback Copies with Expensive Book Covers

Paperback copies yellow, fall apart, or become uninteresting to students very quickly. The time and money invested in fully processing and covering paperback books is not returned. Simply replace paperback copies with other inexpensive copies or purchase the most popular titles with an eBook copy. Public domain titles are free and available on any type of device, and e-titles are normally less expensive than their print counterparts.

Do Minimal Processing and Cataloging to Get Items into Students' and Teachers' Hands as Quickly as Possible

Stamp, create a temporary record, write the barcode on the inside cover, or quickly apply a preprinted dumb label. You can complete the processing and cataloging when the item returns. Responding immediately to your patrons' needs will demonstrate your willingness and ability to give them what they want when they want it. It's good publicity for you and your services, and the free advertising will spread quickly. If you get lucky, the popular books will be constantly out until the day they fall apart, and you will never need to fully catalog them.

Implement On-Demand Purchasing, Acquiring, and Providing That Ensures That Every Item Will Be in Demand

Consider putting off purchasing those best sellers until you know they will be requested and used. In today's world, you can place a book order today and have it tomorrow or the next day. Do the minimal processing and get that item to the patron quickly. How happy is the student or teacher who is handed the material that was ordered just for them? Again, it's our professional purpose to make our patrons happy and fulfill their needs. How many books have you purchased, cataloged, processed, advertised, and displayed in the past school year that have never been loaned? Don't you wish you could have that money back to spend on something else? Only spend on what you know is needed. Wait until a new class is up and running before purchasing a database or items for the associated research. Be certain that there will be research associated with that new class and do some convincing of the importance of the research if there's not. No longer are our library programs judged by patrons, the public, and other libraries, and evaluated by our business managers, boards, and supervisors on the number of books that we have and have circulated. Our role has expanded way past that simple data and statistics; services, instruction, collaborations, and crystal ball reading are the most important responsibilities that should be your focus.

Don't Worry about Beautiful Shelves

Books and spine labels that line up perfectly are not a priority in your life. Sure, you want students and teachers to be able to find an item independently; there is value in shelf-reading, but don't get carried away. Messy shelves usually indicate busy shelves, and that's a good thing. You want your patrons to feel comfortable browsing, pulling, and using items on your shelves. As for meticulous spine labels at a certain height and font, don't waste the time. I was horrified that the library in which I began working had handwritten spine labels in various colors of ink, markers, and handwriting. After my initial year, I decided that my predecessor was right; it doesn't matter. Nobody has developed lifelong learners from perfectly groomed and maintained rows of books. I've long since given up on pretty shelves and spend my time with students and teachers.

Mark Books That You Want Students to Browse with Removable Stickers Instead of Pulling and Reshelving

Encourage your students to go into the stacks and browse. They might find a better resource next to the book that is flagged for their class. Students will begin talking to each other about topics and books as they browse the stacks, and will do some peer-to-peer informal teaching. I always hear, "There's a book right there about that topic," or "I have this book that we can share," or, "Ask the librarian—she always knows."

Or if students don't have time to browse, add the print titles to your research guide or pathfinder so that all of the research resources are together in a single, searchable place.

The time you'll save having students find items for themselves is huge, and again, you can spend that time helping students narrow or focus their topics and reminding them about digital information that might also be of value for the project.

Don't have the time? It's time to make the time to save time. Are you following listserves, blogs, Pinterest, or Twitter to compare what you do with what others do? Are you always actively searching for better ways? This is what keeps us important to the educational process and ready for changing trends.

TECHNOLOGY DEVELOPMENT TOOLS

Those "cannot control" technology changes can be managed by a desire and earnest effort to embrace and develop tech skills. As our tech skills become more advanced, technology becomes more intuitive and natural. Today's learners and digital natives don't have an extra digital chromosome or supernatural ability that we didn't inherit. What they do have is exposure, practice, peer pressure, and natural curiosity.

Allow yourself to succumb to healthy peer pressure; ask your librarian friends about tech workshop, conferences, blogs, books, journals, and organizations that they recommend. Sign up and participate in any workshops or professional development that fit your needs or stretch you a bit past your comfort zone. If you have never tweeted, blogged, or used Pinterest, at least learn why they are so popular. You don't need to commit to using them, but you will learn why so many people depend on them for professional development. Create a Goodreads account and post the books you are reading, and have read, with short reviews. Link your Goodreads recommendations through your library website. Read your print or electronic journal a second time and look closely for terms, tools, and information about technology that you've passed over previously because it's unfamiliar or uninteresting to you. Take a look at what you, in the past, might not have found interesting. Be curious about that which seems to be interesting to others. Stretch yourself. Never say no to your learning.

Library and education conferences are the best for inspiring and energizing participants. I highly recommend attending as many as you are able and presenting a program to share your best ideas. In just a few days of a conference, you can connect and share with colleagues, renew your dedication and inspire your career, and discover and learn endless ways to solve problems or engage your students. Conferences are expensive with loss of work time, transportation costs, registration, hotel rooms, and dining. But still, if at all possible, try to attend one at least every couple of years.

Technology has removed many of the barriers that confront educators regarding professional development. Keeping up with the trends and tools of our profession has never been less expensive or easier. Social tools such as webinars, videos, Twitter, Facebook, and blogs push the information to us. We need only to catch it, interact with it, investigate it, and assimilate it. We don't need to be anywhere at a certain time. We choose when and how to participate.

For example, webinars, one of my favorite methods of keeping up, are perfect for those who have a hard time getting away from school due to time constraints, policies, or money. Webinars are live online discussions or presentations among participants with a common interest. You can choose to participate fully by logging in at the time of the webinar and asking questions or making comments in real time. Or you can register and enjoy an archived copy that you can view at your leisure. You can leave and return to the recorded and archived webinar as often as you like, and rewind to hear or see something again. Webinars usually include audio and visual aids such as PowerPoint slides, website demonstrations, or informational links. Almost daily, I receive announcements of webinars with wide varieties of topics and focuses. Many webinars are sponsored by library and education organizations, and most are totally free. You need only to register and make sure that your computer is equipped with the correct tools for viewing.

HOW'S YOUR ATTITUDE?

The good news is that there are many more areas in your professional life that you can control, and there are methods and ways to deal with the things that you can't control.

Attitude Adjustment

I believe that an attitude adjustment is mandatory for all of us in these transitional times. All of the roles, responsibilities, and tasks that we have assumed in the past, and envision for the future, are sure to be changing. I constantly remind myself not to take my job and myself too seriously. Sure, I'd like to be recognized for the involvement I have with students' successes and learning, and yes, we need to continue to seek respect for the library profession in order for libraries to thrive. But no, there is no job, task, or chore that is beneath me and my level of education.

Take this short, five-question, very unscientific quiz to test how your attitude affects your school life:

> Check the response to the statement that best describes how you have reacted or think you would react to the situation.
>
> 1. **Your new principal informs you in November that there is no more money to spend on discretionary purchases for the library. She defines "discretionary" as popular fiction and prizes for the reading contests that you have been holding for the past decade.**
>
>   _____ You tell her that these purchases support the literacy programming that you provide through the library and hope that she can find a way to provide those budgetary needs so that your students can learn to read.

_____ You don't say anything but stomp back to the library and tear down the signs for the Spring Break Reading Contest. Then you tell students who ask about the signs that the contest is cancelled.

_____ You create a list of popular fiction and nonfiction to request from the public library through your educator's collection card, and you think of inexpensive yet valuable prizes that you can use for the reading contest. Prizes might include:

- Library Get Out of Fines cards modeled after the Monopoly Game pieces
- To the Head of the Line cards for students to jump the line for checking out books or asking questions
- A prize collection of a bookmark, chocolate kisses, and a Library Reading Contest Certificate of Honor and Recognition

2. **Your library's server crashes in March, and no data can be retrieved.**

_____ You don't sign next year's contract and hand in your letter of resignation.

_____ You cry and then yell at the noisy students in the library to shut up.

_____ You cry and then immediately create a checkout list in print or an Excel spreadsheet to manage the current checkouts and returns. Then you begin planning what else you need to do.

3. **Three students fall asleep and one snores during your MLA citing and bibliographies presentation.**

_____ You tell them (when they wake up) that they missed important information that will be on a test and that you are not going to repeat any information or provide any individual help to them.

_____ You show the teacher and class as the bell rings where your online video tutorial about MLA is located.

_____ While you wait for these three students to come to you about the information they missed but desperately need, you update your presentation with a game format that engages and awards prizes to the winners, and you incorporate segments of your online video tutorial into the game for the next time that you teach this information.

4. **While you are in the middle of recording a video tutorial for tomorrow's first period class, a teacher walks into your office and asks you to laminate a poster for her.**

_____ You take a deep breath and tell the teacher that you're happy to laminate the poster, or show her how to do it, as soon as you finish your recording.

_____ You ask her if she has ever experienced someone rudely interrupting her while she is working on a project and offer to laminate the poster when you've finished your project.

_____ You tell her that laminating is not in your job description and that you have a master's degree.

5. **It's time to go home after a long day at school, but an upperclass student is tutoring a younger student in the library, and they don't seem to notice that you're packing up to leave.**

_____ You sigh heavily, turn out the library lights, and stand at the door with you key in hand.

_____ You tell the students that they have 10 minutes to finish up.

_____ You ask the students how much longer they need and tell them that you're happy to stay an extra few minutes.

Okay, perhaps the most appropriate—and inappropriate—choices in the quiz are obvious, but let's be honest with ourselves and admit that we have been tempted to respond in some of the less appropriate ways. Vow never to give into the temptation. One angry word and glare is all it takes to undo the progress you've made in developing a library program that is appreciated and used.

TRANSFORMING: BECOME YOUR AVATAR

It's time to become the interactive resource and tool for students, teachers, administrators, and your community. Avatars aren't confined to the limiting dimensions of traditions and space. Like our avatars, we need to move beyond past traditions, limiting practices, and space of our school libraries. Become a powerful change agent. Speak up and show up. Reinvent yourself and your library program.

I tell teachers whenever I get the chance that I can make their lives easier and less chaotic. I promise them that I will never say "no." I'm happy to laminate items for them, proctor a test, and set up the text to speech feature on our desktops when necessary. And I am eager to act as a PEZ dispenser to distribute class notes or loan textbooks to students in the library on an as-needed basis.

I really am happy to do those things because they require a discussion, explanation, or face-to-face contact with the teacher or student who requests something from me. At that time, I can remind a student of something else I can provide, and talk with a teacher about my ideas for collaboration and library instruction. It works. I've had a few burned fingers from laminating, and a couple of ego bruises from feeling like a clerk instead of a card-carrying librarian, but what matters in the end is that I win the trust of teachers and students—they know that I'm approachable and that I really will do anything for them.

BE PROACTIVE AND FLEXIBLE

Nothing is to be gained by waiting and watching. Don't assume that you don't have any collaborative projects with teachers scheduled today because teachers don't need or want your help today.

Don't wait to be asked. Constantly and continually do the asking, offering, and providing. Make announcements and offers in faculty meetings. Extend your services beyond the norm; solve scheduling problems for administrators and teachers by offering to take a class that needs a sub and use the time to discuss media literacy. Take a captive audience and create a game and prizes that reinforce the research they performed last week for a social studies topic. Don't think of yourself as a sub; recognize how lucky you are to be gifted the extra time to develop your students' skills and abilities.

Provide booktalks and suggestions of books made into movies to a class that suddenly ends up in the library because their teacher went home ill. Have a discussion about their favorite movies and books. Be open, be involved, interact with your students, and stay up-to-date with today's pop culture so that you can relate to their interests.

Lower your expectations of what your responsibilities are. Fix that printer and shelve your own books. Dust if necessary and don't wait for maintenance to rearrange the chairs. Do everything that helps you create what works for you and your patrons.

BE NOSEY

Find out what's happening in the classroom on a daily basis. Match up your library services and resources to enrich classroom discussions and activities. Suggest a video clip that reinforces what students are studying in health class or provide a couple of magazine or journal articles that highlight topics of interest for current events discussion in social studies. What you provide spontaneously and without being asked may not be used immediately or at all. It might not fit into the class time constraints, but you can be sure that the teacher will remember that you provided the resources without even being asked. Your interest in what happens in the classroom will not be forgotten or dismissed.

Be open and flexible with your scheduling. Allow teachers to impulsively bring classes to the library for any reason, even if it's just that their classroom is too hot or too cold. Don't let your disappointment over the loss of a quiet, class-free period that you were looking forward to show on your face. Find a way to make it work and encourage last minutes requests. Some of my last minute requests have morphed into regular and valuable collaborations and relationships with teachers.

HELP OUT

Offer the "I can save you time" promise. Tease, tempt, and solve others' time constraints, and start the "I can, and will, do anything" buzz. Who, in their right mind, would refuse or not want to test these promises?

When you pass a teacher with a frantic look on his face, one who is running to the copier to make three more copies of a test, or one who is trying to figure out how she can both proctor a classroom of students taking a test and provide accommodations to a few students who need extra time and the text to speech feature, solve the time problem. Ask if you can help in any way, offer to make a few copies on the library copier or scanner, and put forth that you are happy to provide the test accommodations for the students who need it. You'll actually use very little of your own precious time, but the memory of how you offered to help will be timeless.

Remind teachers, especially new teachers, at the beginning of the year that you are eagerly awaiting ways to save them time. Provide a list of all of the services and help that you can provide. Send the list to teachers through e-mail, presentations, or in paper format. Follow up by asking teachers to add things that you haven't thought of to the list.

It is not the making copies, proctoring, or subbing that I'm hoping to add to my list of responsibilities and tasks—it's that face-to-face time, trust, reliability, and approachability that I want to develop with teachers.

Students always want to save time with homework and schoolwork, and I promise to teach them efficient and successful methods that ensure an A+ on their assignment. I also add the disclaimer that the quality of the information found and how that information is used and assimilated must also be good to win that A+. I boast about how quickly the best and most reliable information can be found through proprietary databases. I tell students why these resources are password protected and how that makes them valuable jewels locked away from everyday web searchers. I brag about how these databases and the content that they hold are selected specifically for them and the topics that they study in high school. I count off on my fingers the number of steps of review and evaluation that databases go through in order to make student research productive and efficient: from the editor of a publication to their school librarian who chooses the specific database or information to for specific classes, assignments, or students. I tell them that they can search the information fearlessly due to the evaluative and selection process of the databases. I show off a few quick and dirty strategies for a student's topic, and guide them through the results and how they might choose what they need from the long list of most reliable sources.

I remind them that it took only two, three, or four minutes to find one or two items that fit their needs. I ask them to compare this search with a similar search in Google and how many millions of hits they will need to wade through before they give up or find something of little value that their teacher will question concerning credibility or currency.

Although the freshman students all appear convinced at the moment, I know that it will take four years of reinforcement and practice to make them certain that this is a more efficient and better method of finding academic and scholarly information. I am more than happy to spend these years teaching them to save time. And when time is no longer their only concern, they will be open to seeing the value and treasure that reliable research harvests.

GO BEYOND ACADEMICS

Lines blur between school and personal lives in a school setting. It's difficult to know how to limit your role and time, as well as identify and separate your services from those that a public library already provides.

Sometimes we do perform similar or identical roles as the public library, and I want those blurry lines that will keep students and teachers continuing to ask for something from the nearest expert. My greatest hope is that students and teachers find their school library invaluable. I want their heads turned toward the library (any library) and not to Google to find information that could impact their lives and learning. If that involves helping them prepare for a summer service trip or spring break vacation, health and wellness information about their parents' newly diagnosed illness, or how to help their friend find a perfect dog, I'm on board.

Most of our daily interaction with students and teachers is through classes and academic settings, but wouldn't the perfect world include us in personal decision making as well? How easy it is to provide the environmental club with the newest book, article, or activity about recycling and Earth Day, and to hand a group of girls talking about prom dresses the newest *Teen Vogue* or *Seventeen* issues that highlight the season's styles. Be approachable and interested in your students; ask them for recommendations for a gift for your niece and whether they think you'll enjoy the latest movie starring Bradley Cooper.

Broadcast pop culture information to gain students' attention. Display popular movie posters and video trailers to demonstrate that the library goes beyond Shakespeare and the Declaration of Independence. Put your most popular books with information about authors that students recognize at eye level. Subscribe to magazines that entertain them. Stop judging what is or isn't meaningful and important for them to learn. Make your library more than schoolwork and academics.

TAKE A HOLIDAY

I tell teachers all the time that it's a busman's holiday for me to help with their personal research. Help your teachers with their graduate program research or a research study that they want to use in class. Find the articles that they can't locate or help them create a strategy for their research, and find out how valuable you become in both their personal and classroom activities. Not only will you be making new or better relationships with those on whom you depend for collaboration, but you'll also have the opportunity to do some research and skill sharpening beyond the school curriculum.

Work with different age groups when you get the opportunity. Teach a summer technology camp or workshop to lower school or middle school students if you normally work with teens. Work with teens if you normally work with younger kids. It's very energizing (and you'll sleep well at night) to prepare, lead, and interact with other age groups. It's also a great way to audition new media tools and programs that you might want to use in your library or tell teachers about.

I've been "camping" for several years with 7- to 12-year-olds, and after a week or two of helping students spell and watching in awe at how quickly they learn to embed a widget into a webpage or create a stunning Animoto video, I always feel a huge sense of satisfaction and gratitude for choosing the path and career that I have.

Student assistants often help with the programs that I teach in the summer, and I ask them to suggest a media or technology program that they have used themselves. If they are willing, I let them lead that part of the class, and I take the assistant role. It's good for the teens to lead and teach, and it gives me more tools for my toolbox.

I always return to my high school students with a new repertoire of media toys to try with them and a renewed sense of purpose. And I'm also glad that I don't need to walk anyone to the restroom.

SURPRISE THEM

Surprise your teachers and students by telling them that you pledge to "never say no." If you don't know or don't have an answer or resource, you will find out what or how to provide it. Instead of signage with library rules (that no one reads or pays attention to), post signage with your never say no pledge. Don't worry about promising what you can't deliver—you are not promising to know everything and to provide everything, but you are promising to find out how the issue, need, or problem can be solved.

WIN WHEN OTHERS WIN

You will be the winner when you provide opportunities for students, faculty, and staff to win prizes and recognition. A little healthy competition that gives you good press—and reinforces literacy and lifelong learning—cannot be bad. Let your imagination dream up themes, contests, and programming that are interactive and rewarding. Reading contests take very little of your time to create and coordinate, and they recognize those who love to read and who might not be recognized in other areas. Hold the contest over long breaks like summer, spring, or winter and keep it simple. Use the honor system and require little from participants to play; simply ask for number of pages and titles, and trust that their submissions are honest.

Recognize and promote a larger commitment to reading and lifelong learning by creating a book, reading, or literacy award. It could be the century award that recognizes students for reading at least 100 books during their four years of high school, or a quarter-century award for 25 books during a single year of middle school. Again, keep it simple and allow the honor system to monitor the applicants. Make it a big deal and recognize the club members at annual award or academic assemblies.

These reading or literacy recognitions are intended to reward students, but the library program will also benefit from the good will efforts it extends. Your interaction will have impact beyond the library walls, and it will be noticed and appreciated.

HUMILITY

Apologize. Surprisingly, an apology always seems like a big surprise to students. My invisibility cloak immediately falls to the floor and students recognize that I am a human, made of skin and bones, when I apologize. I have lots of opportunity for that to happen. I make lots of mistakes. I try something new and it doesn't work. I'm not always cheerful or high energy. I don't always hide my frustrations and feelings. I don't always leave my personal life at home. And, I don't always have the right and ready answer for my students or teachers. Somehow, an apology makes us more likeable and approachable.

SATISFY ON-DEMAND REQUESTS

Happy students are mobile marketing devices. Word spreads like fire when I solve a student's (usually last-minute) need and download an eBook title to an iPad or book reader. In only minutes, this happy and successful student is on his way with the tool he needs. On-demand items free me from guessing what titles students will want or need, they take no space to store, and they don't need to be shelved when the items are returned. It's a win-win.

ADMIRE YOUR STUDENTS

Think about what students can teach you and how they can influence you. Dig in and free yourself from being the omnipotent being at the head of the room or behind the circ desk. Allow this generation's tech agility and curiosity lead you to a broader understanding and knowledge of technology, popular issues and items, and what makes them tick. Challenge students to question authority, even yours, and to ask, doubt, and evaluate everything that they are told. These foundations are exactly what we need for tomorrow's leaders who will think critically and who will look for evidence to support their views and opinions. Give a prize or award to those who can stump the librarian or provide an original and different strategy during research instruction, or at any time. Or let them bear the title of Library God or Goddess of the Day. The challenge will give your students permission to think beyond what you're teaching, and you are likely to find more strategies, methods, and examples to share with future learners.

CURB APPEAL

Create a space that draws people in. Move furniture and rearrange what your patrons and community have come to expect. Nothing announces change and new beginnings better than the rearrangement of space. At home, in the workplace, and especially in schools, we tread the same paths without really seeing or recognizing what's in front of us.

Shake everyone up and move chairs, benches, and stools to create intimate seating spaces. Buy inexpensive beanbag chairs if you can't afford or don't already have soft and comfy seats on which students can sprawl and relax. Weed your books to the bare minimum and see if you can remove a couple of shelving units to provide more open seating space. Divide your facility into different areas with different purposes.

Create a garden space with a few chairs or a bench near a window and place large, medium, and small plants on every available spot surrounding the garden space. Find, make, or purchase inexpensive garden accessories: birdbaths, birdhouses, a section of picket fence, rocks, sundials, and anything else you can think of to set the mood. Ask the art teacher to provide or help find materials and create a garden sign or plaque that gives credit to the contributors.

Build a quiet study space in a remote area of the library. Just one or two seats will likely suffice. Place some dictionaries, thesauruses, and a mug full of pencils, pens, or markers to create an atmosphere of serious focus. Add a tabletop reading light that can be turned on (or not) for more ambiance.

BOARD GAMES ARE THE ORIGINAL SOCIAL TOOLS

Find spaces where students can gather to visit, or work or play as groups without becoming a distraction to others. Students will likely find these spaces without much guidance, and combinations of soft seating or tables and chairs will satisfy the need and purpose of meeting. Have a collection of board games and jigsaw puzzles along with popular reading materials like fiction, magazines, and newspapers. Don't forget that students love to look through old yearbooks, school papers, and literary magazines. Place crossword puzzles, sudoku, and riddle books nearby that students can discover, pick up, and use. Allow all of these items to be loaned to students and teachers, and consider planning a gaming event for students and teachers or parents to participate in as a community.

Are you wondering how can you add games to your collection when you've spent the last dollar in your budget on an eBook that a student requested? Ask faculty and staff to donate games and puzzles to use in the library. I collected most of our games and puzzle books with a single e-mail request. Teachers love to stop by and see students playing the game that they donated. Take photos of the students playing games and tweet them, pin them on Pinterest, or display them on a library information monitor. Place colorful cards or flyers on tables during free bells that say, "Play Scrabble," "Board Games Equal Social Media," or "Game On. Play a Game." Sometimes a simple invitation to play is all that's needed for students to get started.

PACK UP AND MOVE

Come out from behind the circulation desk and be "among your people." When you experience your patrons from the other side, you will be amazed to realize how much of a barrier the circ desk is between you and your patrons. With my laptop, I moved out from behind my circ desk into my general library space earlier this year and discovered a whole different atmosphere and energy. I move around areas at different times, and I've never had so many impromptu interactions with teachers and students. Faculty and staff stop by to chat or to find out if something is wrong with my desktop computer or chair. Students feel more comfortable sitting down next to me, turning their heads to ask a question, or just asking me how I am. And I'm less likely to become absorbed beyond awareness of what's happening around me. There isn't all that much time to sit and work, but when it arrives, you'll find that you have new and improved presence among your patrons.

POP STARS ARE OUR FRIENDS

Freshmen come into our school new, at the bottom of the student and social hierarchy, scared, worried, and sometimes a little brash. When freshman library and information orientation occurs, they drag into our space expecting a description and demo of the library catalog, information databases, library rules and policies, and anti-Google and Wikipedia propaganda. They do get all of that, but I hide it behind my celebrity friends. I create a game called the Celebrity All Star Game. The game offers prizes for the team that is most successful in finding information about pop stars like Jennifer Lawrence, Miley Cyrus, Taylor Swift, Liam Hemsworth, and Robert Pattinson. I use different scenarios for each research skill to be reinforced: Taylor Swift is worried that her songs and albums are being pirated, and that she won't be able to afford to continue her career. My authentic purpose is to discuss copyright and plagiarism issues. Miley Cyrus asks for the students' help in finding information or articles about women and the media, but my real intent is to teach research skills. By the time students are finished aiding their favorite celebrities, they have learned how to navigate our library in all ways digital and physical with a new respect for copyright, plagiarism issues, and research. Not a bad start for early freshman year.

THROW A PARTY

If you haven't held a new materials fair, schedule one at a time that allows teachers and students time to browse, ask questions, and experiment. Have an open house atmosphere that allows patrons to come and go, staying as long as they like. If your library is used for faculty meetings, you can schedule the fair on a day of a meeting so that teachers can mingle among the resources as they wait for the meeting to begin.

A few days before the event, draw people to it by e-mailing an Animoto video to students and your community that highlights the new resources. Play the video the day of the event on your largest screen in the library to provide atmosphere and a commercial for the event and resources.

Set up desktops, laptops, iPads, and all of your devices with new tools, apps, eBooks, and programs for patrons to take for a spin. Create mini movie type posters to inform what is available on each device.

Set out your newest and hottest print titles for patrons to browse. Provide a section of past favorites or most popular titles from 5- or 10-years ago that will create another round of attention for past favorites.

Offer treats, have background music, and be a gracious host. Don't worry about smudges, crumbs, or dropped iPads or iTouches. It's better to have been used and broken than never to have been used at all. Mingle and talk to your patrons. Discuss how tools and resources, and you, can help them.

BREAK THE RULES

Don't wait for teachers or administrators to send you lists of required summer reading titles. Ask for the lists, find the titles, and purchase a few library copies. Offer these copies to students to take over the summer. Don't take the time to catalog them and don't worry if they come back with sand, water stains, dog-eared, or not at all. It's all in the cost of doing business.

Break the Silence

Have some fun with your space and students. Music Festival Fridays (or Tuesdays, Mondays, etc.) will always turn more than a few heads. On Friday afternoons, if there are no classes scheduled, and students agree, I announce that it's Music Festival Friday. I ask students if they'd like to use their own collection of music, or I play Pandora through the library speakers and my iPod. We don't turn it up enough to rock the building, but it's a treat that many of my students have come to expect. Or break the rules if iPods are forbidden in your school and announce that students are allowed to plug in and use their devices with headphones during a certain time (you know when you need to clear it with administrators). I've had teachers walk by and be drawn into the library to find out what's going on. I've never had a complaint, and I've overheard teachers and administrators talk to others—in positive ways—about our music festival.

Make it clear to students that talking is required in the library. With so much group and team activity, coordination of projects and assignments, peer tutoring and coaching, and daily excitement that includes discussions about classes, events, and life in general, it's hard to imagine a silent, serious, and solemn library space. However, a reminder will always be necessary that the library is a resource for everyone—with individual and rapidly changing needs—and that our rights end where the next person's begins.

ARE YOU A GENIUS?

Do you find esoteric information, images, or articles for patrons? Do you resolve problems of saving, sharing, and connecting? Do you answer a zillion questions daily? Do you occasionally fix computers, printers, and copiers? Yup, you are a genius.

Apple store employees do some of the things mentioned in the preceding paragraph, and they work at the genius bar. That, I guess, makes them geniuses. And since we go beyond what they do, we are uber-geniuses. But, for the sake of humility and collegiality, let's just stick with the term "genius."

You can share your genius status with students or groups of students that sign on to help solve technology problems around the school or library. Create your own genius bar in the library where your patrons can come for technology help. Have a specific hotline through e-mail, a messaging center, a Twitter account, or a phone line for contacting a genius when necessary. And market the program. Announce that everyone's tech problems can now be easily solved and that the geniuses and tech doctors have their backs. To kick off the program, offer chocolate kisses or jellybeans to the first five individuals with problems to be solved. Step away and trust those you trust to take charge. Let your students figure out how to manage complications and problems. Step in only when they ask, or when you see fear or desperation in their faces.

Using students and teens to help is like plugging in extension cords around your building. The reach of the teen's expertise will go farther and further than you can imagine. Peers helping peers, students helping teachers, and teens helping adults are the best ways to build leadership, confidence, trust, and a continuum.

The tech doctors in our school—who are part of a school club made up of members who are usually upperclassmen with a history of dependability, tech interest, and knowledge—check in to find out if there are any problems they can solve. Students use their honor time, or free bells, to schedule or provide impromptu help to teachers, students, and administrators.

This genius bar, the tech doctors, or any other student-led program hands over leadership opportunities to students. They get to feel the accomplishment and satisfaction of helping a classmate, teacher, or even their principal out of a jam, and they get the well-deserved acknowledgment of a job well done. Our students proudly serve our community as tech doctors by satisfying a much-needed role in our school.

Look for opportunities to involve your students and teens in performing jobs that you and others don't have time to do. Honor them, and give them kudos and awards or gifts at the end of their term or year. As their "boss," offer to write recommendations for your best geniuses or doctors for scholarship or college applications.

You never know from where and how the next generation of librarians comes, and you never know if you might be the one to spark that interest and passion.

BE A BRAGGART

One of my least favorite things to do—I'm guessing that it's something most educators and librarians don't have in our genetic code—is to brag about what we accomplish in our careers.

We know we do everything in our job description and much more, and we know that there are many, many details, tasks, and jobs that go unnoticed and unrecognized. And we are okay with that. We earn self-satisfaction and go home at the end of the day or school year satisfied knowing how we impacted young lives.

In the interest of self-preservation, promoting the library profession, creating satisfying evaluations for our job descriptions and positions, justifying budget requests and permission for things slightly outside the norm, and making the road a little sunnier for those who succeed us, we need to shout about and document everything that we do.

Whether your administrator or boss requires or asks you for a report or list of accomplishments on a regular basis, you need to provide a lasting and regularly produced document.

Provide a monthly report form the library that is categorized by duties such as administrative, professional development, instruction and collaboration, meetings and participation, student involvement, circulation data and statistics, and books purchased, acquired, and processed. You can add anything or any category that describes even the smallest tasks that you perform occasionally, just once, or on a regular basis. Have a category for other items that don't seem to fit anywhere else.

A monthly report will also help with time management. You'll begin to see a pattern of how you spend your days, weeks, and months. You'll have a structure for justifying requests and needs for the library. You'll also have a treasure of information for writing a resume or curriculum vitae.

You don't need to start fresh every month with a brand new and original report. Copy and paste the first month's report, and replace the old information with what's new. Use bullet points instead of lengthy explanations. Don't provide too much detail; you want your administrator to read it, not set it aside for later.

At the end of the year, use your monthly reports to create a state of the library report that is a summation of your completed tasks from the monthly reports, and add the details and narrative to make it come alive. Add photos, examples, and quotes from patrons. Post it on your website for the entire community to see. Be transparent, and some sun just might begin to shine on you and your program.

IF IT WALKS, TALKS, AND LOOKS LIKE A LEADER, IT IS A LEADER

Is "leadership" a scary word? Do you worry that taking on one leadership position will lead to another and another? Do you feel you lack leadership skills?

Librarians are natural leaders. For the most part, we work autonomously; work within and balance budgets; develop our own priorities, services, abilities, and programs; and choose resources to best support our curriculum, students, and teachers. Our position requires us to be independent and good decision makers. We work with every person in the school from the incoming freshmen to the outgoing seniors; we provide articles and information for our principals; we work closely with the staff in the business office; we provide teachers with training, media, tech tools, and fresh ideas; and we usually have interaction beyond our school walls with our professional community. We coordinate author visits and programming with public libraries, and we compare prices, services, and advantages of the latest tools. We chaperone field trips, lead retreats and assemblies, moderate clubs, and support student performances. We have a resume that defines a leader.

In order to step into the leadership spotlight, all we need to do is to take these skills, talents, and responsibilities and share them. Go beyond your library and school, and contribute what you can. Get involved. Raise your hand. Join every possible committee and board inside of school and in your professional world. Advocate for libraries, literacy, and educational issues that effect your students and school community. Emily Sheketoff, executive director of ALA's Washington office, advises in the July 20, 2012, AASL Advocacy Tip of the Day: "Don't wait to be empowered, don't wait for someone to ask you about your own experiences. We need to speak up when policymakers discuss issues that we know and care about, be it education, literacy or technology."

Stay local by joining and participating in your region's library consortia, or go national and participate in national organizations like the International

Society for Technology in Education (ISTE) and the American Library Association (ALA).

Involvement in your library profession through volunteer positions is likely to be the most rewarding and valuable professional development that you ever do. You will get to know librarians from all sizes, types, and styles of libraries, and you will broaden your knowledge base with these relationships. You will be energized by lively discussions and debates at meetings. You'll hear and see other sides of the story, expand your view, and—perhaps—change your mind.

If you choose, start out slowly and volunteer at a local conference or workshop. Later, help to develop a local conference or workshop. Before you know it, you'll be asked to run for office, complete the term of a member who is leaving, or serve as committee chair.

All that is truly expected of you, as a leader, is to share. Share your experiences, ideas, thoughts, worries, and time.

Committees and boards aren't for everyone. You might prefer to present at a workshop or conference, or to write and publish an article for a professional journal about your terrific program, service, or idea. Review books and keep those free books for your library. Write a book—find a topic that interests you and develop it. Every book is written one word at a time, and no one has more time than anyone else. Go to meetings. Talk with others just like yourself. Do anything to broaden your perspective.

If personal time permits, volunteer at organizations or small libraries that need help with professional library tasks. Not only will these groups see you as a leader, but they will likely see you as their hero and best friend.

Leadership serves others, but it also serves us. We crash through the walls of our own library, existing knowledge, and experiences, and are no longer that which we were.

The first step is the hardest. The rest will come to you. To get started and to see what types of volunteer leadership positions are available, peruse this partial list of volunteer and advocacy positions from the ALA's Association of American School Librarians (AASL) "Committees, Editorial Boards, and Task Forces." Keep in mind that this is a dynamic list that changes as organizational needs change, and check back regularly to see if the area of your interests and talents needs volunteers. For a complete and up-to-date list with live links, go to: http://www.ala.org/aasl/aboutaasl/aaslgovernance/aaslcommittees/committees

ALA's Association of American School Librarians (AASL) Committees, Editorial Boards, and Task Forces

Advocacy
Alliance for Association Excellence
Association of American University
   Presses Book Selection
Annual Conference
Appointments
Awards Committee and Subcommittees
Best Websites for Teaching and
   Learning
Bylaws and Organization
Intellectual Freedom
Interdivisional Committee on
   Information Literacy
AASL/ACRL

Joint Committee on School/Public
   Library Cooperation
AASL/ALSC/YALSA
Legislation
National Conference
NCATE Coordinating
National Institute (Fall Forum)
Nominating
Research and Statistics
School Library Month
Advisory Groups
Publications
Professional Development

Editorial Boards

Blog
Knowledge Quest

School Library Media Research
Essential Links

Task Forces

Best Apps for Curriculum
Educator Pre-Service
Leadership Development
Planned Giving Initiatives
Quantitative Standards

Retirees
Senior Project/Capstone Projects
Standards and Guidelines
   Implementation

A quick search for volunteer library positions in my home state, Ohio, results in over 23 million hits. The top hits suggest that public libraries and historical societies have many volunteer positions available. Do a quick search for your state or city and see how many organizations are begging for help.

An easy and fruitful method of staying up to date with advocacy issues is to subscribe to the daily email post of the AASL's Advocacy Tip of the Day. You can bookmark the website, but why not let the tips come to you? It is a completely, almost hands-free, way of finding out what others are doing to advocate for their own library programs as well as the library profession. Perhaps you can submit one of your own ideas to the site.

4

Engaging Today's Teens

POP CULTURE

News, technology, music, and celebrities that students care about are your tools of engagement.

King of Pop

The iPad is today's king of pop culture and technology trends. There are many reasons that iPads are so popular, and I know that our students find myriad ways to interact with them. Students want to interact with iPads. I want to interact with students. The obvious choice is for me to interact with students through iPads and any other pop culture device that can enhance their learning and my effectiveness.

There is no ignoring the effect that the iPad has had in today's world. As I write this sentence, Apple has sold over 84 million iPads, and controls the tablet market with no competitor even close. The iPad mini has quickly found its way into students' backpacks. The lower price and higher portability is satisfying a need while providing opportunities for even more consumers. The discussion about which tablet or device is right for a one-to-one program now includes the multiple iPad versions, sizes, and price points.

The effect that the iPad has had is not isolated to computers and mobile devices. This type of device—which has reinvented reading books and magazines, watching videos, keeping up with news, TV, movies, friends, and gaming—is pushing developers to satisfy those interests and needs.

Content that can better satisfy consumers' needs through new formats is emerging at rates that make me dizzy. For education and libraries, both benefits and struggles are infinite—how can schools and libraries afford to follow the trends, and how can they not afford to follow the trends?

Publishers are scrambling to create apps for textbooks, eBooks, and supplemental learning material that dazzle students, teachers, and the public. Most eBooks and digital content is accessible the traditional way by going to databases and websites, but what you get, and get used to wanting through these handheld devices, is the future of publishing. Despite the costs and unappealing licensing complications, colorful and interactive material is becoming academic entertainment and content.

Is academic entertainment bad? Will our students' education and knowledge lack the depth of prior generations? Will they not have the ability to read deeply and to assess and question with critical eyes? From the viewpoint in my library, students are learning much more difficult concepts and content than my children or I did. As school librarians, we should still use the context and structure of an assignment or teaching unit to guide us while teaching information, media, and technology literacy; but if we can interact with students and allow them to enjoy learning, this must be the better way. This is the world our students and we live in. Bring today's academic entertainment into your program, and continue searching for better and newer ways to develop instruction, services, and atmosphere that encourage students to keep learning.

Let's look at some practices, tools, and ideas for helping your teens engage and participate more fully in their learning.

WHAT IS POP CULTURE?

My definition of pop culture, and how the term is used in this book, includes people, events, interests, recreation, technology, books, and trends that appeal and are of interest to the masses, and those things that will define us as a group of people decades from now. We won't distinguish among individual tastes and specific types of media, flavors, or sustainability of trends. If your students, as a group, recognize and have appetites for specific activities, media, or products, those things are, in my opinion, tools that might be exploited fairly and freely for educational purposes.

BE POP CULTURE

There are plenty of ways in which you are already participating, both personally and professionally, in pop cultures and trends of today's world. If you text, message, Skype, or Facetime; play Words with Friends, Scrabble, or Farmville; post and read Facebook walls, Tweet, or read blogs; read books on a handheld device, eat French macaroons and drink skim lattes; see the newest and most popular movies, go to concerts, or go to popular restaurants; drive a hybrid, use a GPS, do yoga, or run marathons; or watch *Downton Abby* or *NCIS*, use SIRI to create tasks or reminders, shop for organic food locally, use a Smartphone, or record TV shows or stream them from Netflix or Hulu, you are pop culture. In some not so distant time, a graduate student in sociology will no doubt count you as one of the millions and billions of people in the early decades of the 2000s who participated in the trends of the early twenty-first century.

It seems as though it's harder to keep pop culture out of your library program than it is to invite it in. The everyday things that you participate in can be utilized to connect with teens and bring attention to programs, resources, and services. Take advantage of the social media that you're using for personal purposes and bring it into your program.

All the tools that our students love to use and all of the discussions that they have when they don't know we are listening are usually about pop culture. Taylor Swift, the Hunger Games trilogy, iPads, Xbox, Wii U, *Dancing with the Stars*, fashion, sports heroes, models, and popular activities are examined constantly in our school's halls, classrooms, and library.

Do we see pop culture as a swiftly moving current that washes trends away as quickly as they emerge? Does the rapid speed at which celebrities come and go, how quickly devices replace earlier versions, and popular restaurants and food that come and go make you want to ignore these trends and dismiss their value?

If you do ignore items most teens and the general masses enjoy and on which they place value, you are missing out on tools and opportunities that might better influence and engage students, and help them retain information and knowledge longer and better. I've happily watched students move from bored to eager when some competitive or pop culture additions are built into instruction. I've witnessed races to the newest issue of *Seventeen* and *Mental Floss*, I have been thanked endlessly for providing copies of the newest and hottest YA books, and I've had feedback from teachers who indicate class participation is higher when library instruction includes pop culture themes or game formats.

Students are capable of more than being trend followers, and when you pitch the efficiency of better research skills and the certain success for students who take the time to develop and use good tools and strategies, they will eagerly tune in. Appeal to your students' desire to achieve, and provide examples about how much faster and more successful they will be when they are learning and using the research skills that experienced researchers use. To subtly teach and demonstrate how students can be successful, share personal experiences that demonstrate how you also struggled with research and writing in high school or college. For example, you might describe how in college, after many late nights, stressful efforts, and being close to tears, you finally dragged yourself to the library and humbly asked a librarian for help in locating needed information. Explain how you discovered in a single night how that one location—a library—is a one-stop-shopping site for academic information and help. Or share your high school story about how the research topic you chose was a personal interest topic that you were determined to write about despite your frustrations in not being able to find enough information to support your thesis. Explain how your wise teacher reminded you that you don't have to "marry" a topic for a research paper and that you don't even need to believe in your thesis statement as long as you can and do support it successfully in your paper. Your own high school teacher may have reminded you that no one was going to grade you or ask if you truly believed in the statement you wrote.

It's a given that students want to spend less time on homework and that they are probably apprehensive when beginning a new research project. I always ask at the beginning of an instruction session, "Who loves research?" and "Who always finds what they need easily and quickly?" I always get wary smiles, snickers, and in general, negative responses. I then promise I'm not trying to turn them into librarians, but I am going to try my best to convince them that research is fun and similar to solving a puzzle and that they will, through this session, learn about the best research secrets. Teens love puzzles, fun, and secrets, and they love the idea of saving time and effort.

The following sections provide some samples of how pop culture can be used in information literacy or teen programming to relate directly to teens' tastes and interests.

GAMES, POP STARS, AND MEDIA LITERACY

Celebrities are likely to have the most influence on teens outside of their peer group. Teens dress like, gossip about, and are drawn to their favorite celebrities through radio, TV, social media, magazines, clothing and accessories, and movies and concerts. To take advantage of the season's or year's most popular faces, I constantly update the celebrities that I use in my games. And I give myself artistic license to go beyond real people to also include fictional books, TV, and movie characters.

I make the celebrities that teens admire my allies by bringing them into our library and programming. As described in Chapter 3, the freshman orientation the Celebrity All Star Game is structured around the fictional informational needs of pop stars. Students are charged with finding information that pertains to stars' tours, intellectual property, hometowns, personal interests, and careers.

The game is structured differently every time I update it, which is usually once a year. However, if I use the game with a class and sense that it needs improvement, I'll make quick changes before the next class arrives. For example, it's possible that a star that I think is popular with teens is passé or too young or too old to interest a particular group, or I might make a mistake about a name or connection to the star. If you see eyes rolling, feel the giggles mounting, or a student is brave enough to correct you, laugh about your error, joke that you wanted to see if anyone caught it, and change the mistaken material right after that class. Remember our earlier discussion in Chapter 3 about appearing vulnerable and human? Students will appreciate your ability to recover and admit your error.

Use this blunder to ask students to provide a better example for the task and then assimilate that into your updated game. It's just another method of students teaching students and learning to share opinions and information, and your teens will love to know that you used their idea (even if you have to tweak it a bit). And to develop a task that might stump their classmates, they will need to think critically and develop a better understanding of intricate search details.

Take a look in the following text at how a game might be structured with some examples from the Celebrity All Star Game.

The freshmen enter the library and sit wherever they like. The students are then broken up into teams by counting off into the number of teams that I want or need. I try to keep my teams small so that each team member can participate fully and for the practical reason that prizes for the winning team can get costly with larger teams. A team with four or five members usually works well.

For this type of situation, I'm likely to have created a PowerPoint or Prezi presentation that serves as a structure and visual for my presentation and game. I move to my "Rules of the Game" slide and reinforce the rules stated on the slide.

After we go over the rules, the next informational slide with images of the stars that we are helping appears, and I begin to explain the premise of the game. I say that to help the stars find the information they want and need, we must research both efficiently and effectively. A discussion begins to brainstorm ideas about what might be important when looking for information. For example, I might ask the class for examples or a definition of scholarly information. If no hands are raised (or you can use game clickers or clicker apps instead), I offer bonus points to get the discussion started. Unless the first answer is exactly correct with no opportunity for improvement, I offer more bonus points for anyone who can build on that response or give a completely new and original answer. We then move on to the challenge slides that prompt students to begin a research task for a celebrity. Along with the research challenge, each task slide indicates how many points the correct answer or task is worth.

As students respond correctly or find solutions or information to meet the challenge, they are awarded point coupons. The competitive spirit is likely to

Rules of the Game slide

engage at this point—occasionally, every hand in the room will go up, and I will end that round when the answer is exhausted or time restraints dictate by stating, "One more answer before we move on."

I then proceed to the next slide. For example, a slide might use the *Modern Family* TV series to present a need for finding information about nutritious food. Gloria is an excitable and fast-talking star of the show, and her extended family wants her to modify her diet and eat food that will calm her and make her mellower. The slide instructs the teams to use a specific consumer or professional health database, and to build a search strategy that uses the best terms and methods likely to result in reliable information that satisfies our information need. I might specify that at least two keywords or subject terms must be combined within an advanced search and that we are searching only journals and magazines more current than 2005.

After the teams provide the information, I direct them (for bonus points) to demonstrate how to limit the last response and strategy to a specific magazine or journal. You can switch up the task by asking students to explain how to limit their search to newspapers or peer reviewed journals.

Need a quick and easy bonus question to tag on to the challenge about health or nutrition? Ask why we might restrict the search to 2005 or later, or what is an example of a primary source; acceptable responses to the question might be a brochure from a doctor's office, a food-packaging label, a TV or radio announcement, or an audio podcast or interview from First Lady Michelle Obama about children and nutrition.

Don't forget that research and media literacy is just one part of students' purpose in the library and include information about optional media tools that they can use to complete assignments or projects. A challenge that I include in the All Stars game asks students to choose from a list of presentation tools that Emma Watson might use to create a 20-minute presentation for her community about global warming. Choices include PowerPoint, Prezi, HelloSlide, and Knovio. Chances are that most students won't know about all of those programs, and the discussion will give you a chance to describe or demonstrate, and compare and contrast them for students.

Keep the information that teens are learning about research and media literacy relevant to both their personal and academic needs. Continually compare and contrast how this information or a particular search strategy might aid them in finding help with a personal issue or school assignment in a different class. I always remind them that the skills they just demonstrated by searching a database or catalog for a topic will be transferred to another topic for another need at another time. And the more they practice these skills, the more intuitive and easy they will become.

An early task in your game might be helping students develop skills to choose appropriate sources to search. Ask students to examine a list of your available databases (with or without descriptions) and have teams determine which database(s) might be most likely to provide specific information or articles related to a certain topic. At every opportunity, point out the similarities and differences among databases and sources. Describe how some databases focus on literature or history information and how and why you might find literature information in a history databases, or history information in a literature database, and how some databases seem to cover all fields of study, and others focus on controversial topics and current events.

Offer a current event or pop culture topic to students so that they can practice comparing and contrasting databases or other information sources. For example, you might use "head injuries and athletes" to demonstrate how you can find the following:

- Both scholarly and overview or general information in a single science database
- A current issues resource that provides different points of views and controversies
- How information about head injuries and athletes is likely to be available in many formats, including print, video, audio, and images

When you are fairly certain that the class understands the differences and similarities among databases and sources, move on. This might also be a good time to provide students with needed usernames and passwords for specific sources for their research assignment.

Easy modifications can be made for hands-on classes when students have access to laptops, iPads, or other devices, or as a simple interactive presentation style for classes that are not equipped with devices. You can create tasks that require students with devices to actually search specific databases or sources to find articles and information. For example, you might ask students who have devices to find an article in a health-related journal that discusses a connection between food and emotions or health. For students who do not come with devices, simply create questions or tasks that require students to determine a response, strategy, or answer from the information that you present to them on the slide. For example, connect to your catalog and display it live on your screen or smart board. Then ask students to provide the terms, punctuation, and limiters necessary to create a strategy to find information about the connection between food and health. Ask for a volunteer to enter the information students provide or, for the sake of efficiency, do it yourself. Actually run the search so that the class can reap the reward of seeing their results listed before them.

Another early and important task relates to creating good research topics from the broad topics that many teachers assign with the expectation that each student will narrow the topic to one of their choosing. The following example will work for a class that comes equipped with devices or one without devices. You might begin by saying, "Your teacher has assigned the topic of nutrition to your team, and you must report to the class about how nutrition impacts humans' lives. How might you take the broad topic of nutrition and narrow it to a good research topic?"

Explain the important process of creating a topic that is neither too broad nor too specific, and emphasize that the topic should also be one that classmates and the teacher will find interesting, and makes the student—the researcher— curious. If students stare at you as if they don't have a clue about what you mean, give an example. You might say, "Think about the topic of nutrition. Does that topic inspire you?" As they all shake their head no, start sharing narrower topics and terms that they are all familiar with such as Olympic athlete performance and nutrition, obesity, anorexia, bulimia, pink slime, high sodium and fat, food deserts, and more. Be graphic and dramatic, and try for some "yucks," "icks," or "wows" to get students invested in the discussion and topic.

Describe the big nutrition topic as a huge puffy cloud with smaller and more specific topics made up of the terms "pink slime," "obesity," "anorexia," and "athletic performance" that rain out of it. Ask the class to provide more terms

Table 4.1

Help students develop good research topics

Broad Topic	Advertising	Bullying	Terrorism
Less Broad Topic	Television Advertising	Cyber Bullying	Anti-American Sentiment
Narrower Topic	Alcohol Advertising on Sports Television	Social Networking Sites	Homeland Security
Research Topic	Teens Are Influenced by Alcohol Advertising while Watching Sports Television	Are Social Networking Sites Harmful?	The Patriot Act

related to nutrition and ask them, "Now do you think the nutrition topic can be interesting?"

Walk the class through more examples of developing a research topic from broad to narrow, or create and display a set of examples of broad topics, narrower topics, and good research topics (see Table 4.1) so that the students can see patterns of how narrowing topics can occur. Post your examples on a research pathfinder or guide, or on your webpage. And remind students that they can use this method of creating a research topic in any class or field of study.

Once again, compare the process of research to solving a puzzle—you begin with lots of pieces like topics, information resources, personal opinions, research tricks and tips, and teacher's expectations and guidelines. Then, like a puzzle, the process narrows and focuses to find and organize patterns and similarities. And finally, after much searching, re-searching, and critical thinking, the informational need is on its way to becoming solved and assimilated into an assignment or project.

During the game, be flexible in accepting students' responses and answers. Provide positive reinforcement, and if the outcome is not exactly what you want or are hoping to have students understand, ask leading questions or give clues to help students finally discover the better response. If necessary, backtrack a bit and use another example or explanation. Keep in mind that the goal is knowledge and that the more students stumble and then finally learn, the more they will likely retain.

Let's look at another example of helping a celebrity with her information need. Jennifer Lawrence, star of *The Hunger Games*, wants to invest her hard-earned money and build a modern house to live in with her family. We begin by brainstorming with the class what we already know (if anything) about modern houses, and we look for keywords or ideas that will eventually develop a good search strategy.

I announce to the students that I'm going to use Google and Wikipedia to get us started in our quest for general information about modern architecture—they usually appear to be unsure or wary abut these sources. I ask the class who else would begin their search with Google or Wikipedia. Most raise their hands, and I tell them that I also use Google hundreds of times a day but never for information that I need to trust or rely on for important things like school, career purposes, or to help a friend like Jennifer Lawrence. I tell them that despite what I just said, Google and other search engines are great for getting things started, for example, finding vocabulary and terms to use for a topic. This is also a good time to demonstrate how inefficient the process of searching with search engines is. Do a search and point out how the simply worded search of "modern architecture" on Google results in over 29 million hits, most of which—after a quick scan—appear to be books, furniture, or accessories to purchase from on-line stores. Demonstrate a better search that adds the word "history" and scan the results, pointing out or asking students to grab terms that might be useful search words for modern architecture, for example, "modernism," "mid-century modern," "Eames," and "Frank Lloyd Wright."

At this stage, with the students' suggestions, begin building a research strategy beyond a Google or Wikipedia search to find useful and reliable information about modern architecture in databases or the library catalog. Discuss the steps, choices, and evaluation of resources that are necessary to find the information that will eventually be handed off to Jennifer.

Game tasks can be as general or as specific as you need them to be. To create a challenge with very specific elements, you might charge students to use an advanced search strategy with at least one Boolean operator, truncation, and punctuation that is limited to a full text search of a database. Depending on the specific class and students' engagement or ability level, you can offer bonus points for better and more original strategies.

A third example involves Katy Perry. Require students to determine where and how to find information about the possibility of a hurricane in Florida. The urgency is that Katy Perry is planning a concert next September but is worried about weather issues. This task works well with students who do not have devices available for hands-on exercises. The question requires students to choose from the three possible points to develop a research topic that would likely result in a search strategy that will find the information she needs. Here are the choices for a research topic:

1. The hurricane season along the Atlantic Coast is growing longer.
2. More data is needed to determine the likelihood of a hurricane in a warming environment.
3. Southern states are still cleaning up and making repairs after Hurricane Katrina.

Not only do teams and students need to choose an answer, they also need to present a logical explanation. Ask if anyone can think of another appropriate response and be sure to offer more points for teams that create an original and useful response.

For classes with devices, the challenge can be to have students find data or an article from a scientific journal or magazine about hurricane forecasting.

With all challenges, partial points might be awarded for partial answers. An additional rule that I try to stick with in order to have participation and engagement from each student is to require that each team member respond at least once during the game. Teams can work together to determine an answer or response, but each person much present or speak up for the team. Again, stay flexible. Be creative and target topics and news that you hear students buzzing about in your school.

Occasionally, the winning team is determined almost from the beginning of a game, and other teams begin to put less effort in their responses as they see that they don't have a chance to win. You can rebalance the playing field by asking pop culture questions that anyone can easily answer, for example, "What's the sequel to Veronica Roth's book *Divergent*?" "Where is Lady Gaga's hometown?" or "What's the actor's name who plays Axel in the TV show *The Middle*?" Announce that students can find the answers by using a device (if available) or by collaborating with members of their team. Just make sure that you know the answers to the questions you ask in case no one finds the answer or there is a disagreement about the response.

NOT JUST FUN AND GAMES

The search topics that I present to students always require refined search strategies and information literacy skills, and I add as many photos and images of the stars and their fictional informational needs in order to keep the students engaged with helping the celebrities. Students learn, relearn, and reinforce skills while playing the games, and they learn how to develop the following in each game they play:

- Strong research topics
- Advanced search strategies with keywords or subjects
- Methods of using Boolean operators
- Tools for limiting search results to scholarly material or a specific journal
- Critical thinking skills that determine which information sources and resources are best and most appropriate for the specific information need
- A logical and thorough review and evaluation of the information found

Throughout the game and instruction, we talk as if we truly have been given an assignment from the specific celebrities. It's so much fun to hear a class or

Celebrity All Star Game

5 Points

Point coupons are valuable treasures

team debate which strategy, database, or information is best. For one short period of time, we are friends of the stars, and we want to come through for them. As I've discovered the hard way, it's always best to use celebrities, TV shows, movies, and books that are currently running and very popular. It's not uncommon for young teens to have never watched a *Twilight* series or Harry Potter movie, or to have read one of the books. Today's teens were very young when those titles first arrived on the scene. In addition, students are encouraged to be selective and cautious before submitting the information to their celebrity friends—good results are essential to keeping their favorite celebrities happy and healthy.

To recap, in order to please their favorite celebrities, students and teams earn points for each carefully constructed strategy, correct answer, or original answer. Some points are easy to earn and some are difficult, and students are assigned points accordingly (see an example of the point coupon above). When I see students struggling or drifting away from the activity, I throw out bonus points with random questions to pull them back in. I structure the game to progress in complexity, and by the time we get to the final question, teams are usually asked to perform and demonstrate a series of research decisions, strategies, and searches. Sometimes we run out of time, which is usually because the students are engaged and eagerly trying to earn more points and toss out more answers. Running out of time isn't a big deal, and it's probably better than running out of challenges for students who are engaged in the game. Keep an eye on the clock and announce when it's time to count points. Ask which group thinks it won and then if anyone else can beat that number. Give out the prizes and if time permits, have the students collate the point coupons for you.

MORE POP CULTURE

There are so many ways to incorporate pop culture and so many educators that share their creative ideas.

FOR IMMEDIATE RELEASE: STUDENTS DISCOVER A LOVE FOR WRITING

Peter Gutierrez—a former middle school teacher and author of the blog Connect the Pop: At the Intersection of Pop Culture, Transliteracy, and Critical Thinking—encourages educators to use pop culture for teaching media literacy. He endorses using "fun" strategies to connect with students, and in the August 10, 2012 post "Pop Culture Press Releases: Use These Real-World Models as Prompts to Writing and Critical Thinking," Gutierrez provides a number of engaging ideas to tap into pop culture via the entertainment industry's marketing strategies in order to develop students' critical thinking and writing skills. Gutierrez states that students using their own creativity and writing their own press releases "can anticipate/predict some of the content (using existing teasers, book trailers, etc., for clues), summarize it, practice efficiency/brevity in writing … and perhaps later compare how their made-up press releases compare to the real thing." Take a look at Gutierrez's post and either use the templates he provides or build your own based on his methods.

Imagine the buy-in from middle and high school students when they are allowed and encouraged to use real-world information and pop culture to fuel their creativity to write and think critically. Subscribe and follow Gutierrez through his blog and Twitter (https://twitter.com/Peter_Gutierrez) to discover more methods of using pop culture as a tool to connect with students.

The opportunity to introduce and reinforce the latest library services, features, and resources, as well as new ways to do the same and traditional things, is simple and perfectly matched to the gaming tasks. For example, when challenging students with finding a book through your catalog, change it up and require them to find the book through the your library's catalog app on a handheld device or alternative link from your webpage or pathfinder. If the class doesn't have devices available, demonstrate the information on one that you provide.

Encourage students to constantly think of better and different ways of doing the same things. For example, when students are likely to assume that a database search is going to be run on a computer or laptop, throw in a roadblock and require students to find an alternative method to run the search. Have some iPod Touches, iPads, tablets, and smart phones on hand to loan to teams.

Constantly market your library programming and services within any game at any time. Toss bonus questions out for students to answer or build them into the game structure, asking, "When you don't know where to begin, or are stuck and don't know what to do next, what library resource is always available for help and advice?" Of course, the correct response is you (a librarian) or a teacher. It doesn't hurt to continually reinforce the idea that you are the number one most readily accessible and eager app in the library. Promote an upcoming program or contest and create a game challenge by asking students to respond to questions such as "What is the date for the Banned Books Read-in?" or "Who was the top winner of the Winter Break Reading Contest in either the teacher or student category?" Students can't get too many reminders of resources, programming, strategies, and skills. The more they get, they more they will retain and use again.

Library orientations are not the only opportunity for using games in your instruction. They can be easily built around a traditional research project. For example, I've used a Shakespeare research project as the structure of a *Dancing with the Star*'s library game. The stars are Shakespearean characters and literary critics, and we "dance" through different common themes of Shakespeare's works while locating reliable literary criticisms and background information. Points are awarded for a variety of factors or qualities of answers. Students receive points based on technical execution (effective use of punctuation and Boolean operators), for style (well-developed terms and keywords), and overall performance (good and appropriate results). In addition, clear explanations and justifications of the strategies receive bonus points. Working together with team members is an essential requirement of the game. Each team member needs to participate fully by responding for the team at some point during the game, or they risk points being deducted. Students are reminded that contestants can't dance alone.

I use images of dancing couples to create the challenge slides and paper point coupons, and I pepper my presentation with the current season's *Dancing with the Star*'s dancers, judges, and music. Students love the fun, and I don't ever need to ask them to pay attention. And you would think that the small candy prizes I award to winning teams were crystal trophies.

If students come with iPads, tablets, or other mobile devices, or if you can make at least a few (enough for one per team) available during your instruction, include some apps in your game to make certain that students understand how the different access methods and formats of finding and using information can have the same or similar results as traditional methods of access. In other words, don't forget to include the latest methods of information retrieval in your information literacy instruction. For example, the free SoundHound is a music recognition app that identifies music sung, hummed, or played through speakers. Artist information and song lyrics are also available for most music, and students will love using the new and cool app to discover information about the Beat Generation as part of a contemporary literature or history research project. Or use SoundHound during a pop culture–themed game—for example, the Celebrity All Star Game—that you create to teach information literacy. Pose a challenge to students to find the lyrics for a song that you play aloud for a few seconds. Suggest two modes of searching: (1) the SoundHound app and (2) a website (for those who already know the song and artist). Require the date of the song release and the name of the songwriter and music production company.

Challenge #10

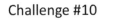

Find a scholarly article in the Journal, *Shakespeare Quarterly,*
that discusses Shakepeare's female characters in Macbeth.
8 points

A *Dancing with the Stars* challenge

Make sure that you choose a song in which students have some interest and replay the song until the first team is successful in finding it on the app. Encourage students to then check a reliable music industry source—discuss what is considered a reliable source—to compare the results found. Finally, remind the class to always question and evaluate the results from any source for reliability and accuracy. In addition, a discussion of the music industry and all the options to access and use music is a great opportunity to discuss copyright and piracy issues. When students consider their favorite musician's interest in royalties and his or her ability to make a living through music, copyright laws and regulations might seem a bit more reasonable.

Another suggestion for integrating mobile devices and their apps into your instruction is to use the free app Epicurious by Conde Nast Digital for students to find a healthy recipe for one of the celebrities that you use in your game. Students can search by browsing categories or by typing in ingredients or key words such as "healthy" or "vegan" to find a match. Encouraging students to use popular apps that aren't necessarily marketed as educational will help them understand that many informational tools or sources can be used for many different purposes as long as they pass the reliability test. We want our students, outside of the school walls, to continue to question and think critically about all information, whether its purpose is academic or personal.

It's likely that some students will be absent on your library game day and that some students might benefit from a review or hearing your presentation again. It's easy to turn your game and presentation into an online tutorial by using media tools such as Jing, Knovio, or Screencast-o-matic. These screen recorders allow you to narrate while moving through your presentation, and if you choose, you can even add a video of yourself via your webcam. Or use Mentor-Mob, one of the newest and most exciting programs I've discovered to create visual playlists from websites, documents, photos, and articles. MentorMob also provides a quiz tool that makes the demo or tutorial interactive. See Chapter 7 for more information about these resources.

BE FLEXIBLE: GAMES ARE NOT FOR EVERYONE

The interactive games aren't appropriate for every situation and group, and I try to carefully determine which classes and students are best suited for this type of instruction. Sometimes, just the straight facts and resources via an informational style of instruction are a better fit for stressed upperclassman working on a serious research paper, and I respect their need to cut to the chase. Or it might be that my own schedule won't allow for the instruction to last the entire bell, and I will decide not to play the game with that class. I can glean useful information when there are groups that have and groups that haven't had the game instruction; compare the control group with the others and discover how much benefit there is in making the instruction fun and interactive.

POP CULTURE ATMOSPHERE IN THE LIBRARY

The next time you visit the mall, grocery store, or any shopping venue, pay attention to marketing devices that depend on and use pop culture to sell to consumers. You'll see and feel energy from familiar faces, movies, TV shows, and technology tools—all advertised in a zillion ways. Think about how you can give your space and program a lift by adapting your marketing and public awareness of services, materials, and programming in ways similar to those you see out in the bigger consumer-focused world.

SOCIAL MEDIA TOOLS

Use pop culture tools and social media to market your library program, services, and resources. Announce that the next 10 students and next three teachers who follow the library's Twitter account, or who like you on Facebook will win a prize. Start tweeting or posting new popular book titles that have just arrived. Offer pop culture trivia questions and award the first correct responder with recognition in a tweet or on Facebook. Before class assignments and project deadlines, tweet the offer of 30 minutes of free and uninterrupted research help to the first responder, and tweet and post the winner on your digital display in the library.

Make announcements to the entire school about the winners and upcoming contests.

When using social media, you'll want to carefully craft your approach in order to connect with as many of the followers you are hoping to reach. There have been studies on how to successfully tweet as well as use Facebook and other social media in a professional setting. Librarians who serve teens have even more issues to consider due to their age and our professional relationships with them and school. You will need to consider if you want a single account aimed at the entire school community and colleagues beyond the school, or if you want separate accounts for students, teachers and administrators, and library colleagues and profession. And you should question, before you set up your accounts, whether you have time to keep up with all of them and post frequently enough to make the tool worthwhile. Consider the following tips and tricks for making certain that your social media has a positive and successful impact on your followers and audience:

1. Know the platform and how it works.
2. Identify your audience and set your goals and objectives.
3. Offer original ideas—or at least original reactions to others' ideas.
4. Don't get into online debates or arguments; take it offline or not at all.
5. Watch your grammar and punctuation, and never use texting jargon. Write as though your high school English teacher is following you.
6. Contribute regularly and steadily. Don't disappear for weeks at a time, and don't bomb your followers with multiple posts at a time. A new post usually dismisses the former post in the mind of followers.
7. Use images or photos when appropriate. A visual is always welcome.
8. Add your photo to your profile. If you just can't do that, add an avatar or other image to represent you. People are drawn to faces and want to know what you look like.
9. Be timely.
10. Ask questions.

Spreading the word of upcoming programs and events in the library is easily accomplished by creating video podcasts or commercials, and by posting them to your social media accounts. If you're camera shy and don't want to star in your own video podcast, you can recruit a few students or collaborate with a technology or broadcast class. Many students love to be in front of cameras, especially when there's not a live audience. Create a script and carefully direct the video or you'll end up with giggles, shaky motion, and not much content. Or give a teacher your script or plan and offer the class free license to be as creative as they like. Embed the video into your webpage and send an e-mail, tweet, or Facebook message with a link to the video. Almost any smart phone or tablet has video capability, so you don't need a video camera to get the job done. Use still or screen shots of the video to create movie posters to place around the school. Posters can be created inexpensively with a number of online poster-making sites. Use Big Huge Labs to create movie style posters (http://bighugelabs.com/poster.php/). Or give Block Posters a try. The site offers a variety of sizes of posters that can be printed out on a regular printer with plain paper (http://www.blockposters.com/). Or just use any word processing program to create a colorful advertisement or poster. You can take screen shots of any of your completed posters or documents and use that image to post to Twitter, Facebook, or Pinterest, or attach the image to any e-mail or other message to send to your patrons and customers.

HUMOR HAS JUST ENTERED THE BUILDING

Your entire school community will benefit from humor that you display and use in your library. There are many sources of educational and library cartoons and comics, and what can be better than having a bad day's craziness softened by something that makes us laugh? Cartoonists are often more than generous with their work by allowing it to be used freely (with credit provided with each use) in schools and libraries. The following text presents a couple of my favorites.

Andertoons (http://www.andertoons.com) by Mark Anderson is a collection of cartoons that covers just about any topic you can imagine. My favorite Andertoons categories focus on technology, education, and teachers. These single-frame comics provide such a sublime and realistic report on the culture in today's schools that I feel like Mr. Anderson must have some underground source of information about schools, students, and teachers in order to hit issues so precisely. Recent themes of Andertoons comics include iPods and iPads, and a contemporary teacher's preference for lattes instead of apples. One cartoon shows a student being instructed by his teacher to write his name on the board, and the caption states, "Before I write my name on the board, I'll need to know how you're planning to use that data." Besides the humor, what I love most about this site is that you can embed the daily cartoon into your website to share with all of your school community or, if you prefer, you can join the e-mail list and the current comic will show up in your inbox on a daily basis. Also, Mark Anderson is happy to make his work available to educators for a very nominal fee or perhaps even without a fee, if the individual contacts him and asks very nicely.

I've used the Unshelved (http://www.unshelved.com) strip by Gene Ambaum and Bill Barnes in my library displays for years. Just as you would expect a couple of funny guys who obviously love libraries and books to be generous to all, they very kindly permit and encourage their works to be shared in all libraries. Unshelved, whose setting is a public library, offers hilarious views—and at times satire—of librarians and library patrons dealing with outdated library and workplace traditions and rules. School libraries will especially appreciate the Unshelved Book Club comics that are full page and in color.

"You don't need to check in on Foursquare, my attendance sheet works just fine."

Cartoons lighten the mood

The Unshelved Book Club comics run on Fridays and again, librarians are encouraged by Ambaum and Barnes to use them in their buildings to promote reading. In addition, libraries, nonprofits, and bookstores are permitted to run comics in newsletters within certain parameters. With permission, followers can use the strips in presentations, posters, and handouts.

If you have students who love graphic novels or comics, especially reluctant readers and writers who love comics, provide students or their teachers with information about how they can practice both reading and writing skills while having a blast using Make Beliefs Comix (http://www.makebeliefscomix .com). This free site requires no download and takes just seconds to get started. Students can choose the number of panels they wish to use, select a character from a cast of many that express different moods, type original dialogue into talk or thought balloons, and add many other details and features. And the original comics can be printed, or saved as an image through a screen shot or clip. Bill Zimmerman, the creator of Make Beliefs Comix, also provides writing prompts for inspiration in his blog. Google's The Literacy Project: Innovative Projects named Make Beliefs Comix as one of the most innovated websites in fostering literacy and writing.

MIX IT UP WITH TEACHING STYLES

The age of the sage on the stage is past. Try something new for fresh results.

Students Teaching Students

Whenever possible, let your students take on teaching roles and teach each other. Students learn better and more when they are involved in the preparation, critical thinking, and processing of information that is required for teaching. Students enjoy changing it up and moving to the front of the classroom, and a possible benefit is that peers (usually) help their friends out by being more attentive and participatory than normal. Play the role of consultant, ready to help and to interject when needed.

Don't miss opportunities to ask for students' help and advice. While teaching or working with a group, ask for an idea or another method that has worked for them. Ask students about programs, apps, and media that they use, and let them demonstrate what they know about them. Ask them to present good ideas as well as tech knowledge and tools to a wider audience—for a faculty meeting, department meeting, or an after-school tech workshop for both students and teachers.

Create a group or club of student tech leaders who are interested in providing service to younger students or older adults in your community. Our school has a student club that provides service and programming in and out of our school. Our club members provide a tech-mentoring program in the fall with fourth graders from local schools. We meet with the fourth graders six times for an hour once a week, and our high school student leaders do it all—they develop, plan, present, and teach the younger students. The first five sessions take place in the computer lab at one of the elementary schools, and we bring the fourth graders to our high school for a party and the final session. The fourth graders love the interaction with the older high school students, and they are eager and completely engaged in the sessions. In the spring, the club offers three sessions of Technophobia: Get Over It to senior citizens that take place in our own high school computer labs. Again, students plan, lead, and teach the workshops, which cover topics such as Facebook, e-mail, and Internet safety and etiquette. In the third and final session, participants are provided opportunities to play with iPads, learning about their functions and features. We pack the house with the workshops and have constant calls to provide even more sessions. And again, our students lead the sessions. Our teen club members don't realize it, but they are developing lifelong skills and abilities through the development, planning, and teaching of these service programs. Meanwhile, the fourth graders and older adults are benefitting from our energetic high school students' personal attention, knowledge, and skills.

Student Tech Stars

Let your student tech stars shine and share their skills and abilities beyond clubs and groups. If one or two students demonstrate interest and advanced technology skills, collaborate with them to create and provide quick tech workshops for teachers, students, or both. Sometimes a 10- or 15-minute window of time will be plenty for these student tech wizards to help others with their iPads, smart phones, Google Drive, or Dropbox. Try creating sessions with specific topics, or, have a The Help Desk is Open event for students to ask questions or get help with random problems. If the student-led events catch on, try to schedule them on a regular basis so that it becomes a regular service for your community. Don't forget to show appreciation to the students who share their knowledge and skills. Small end-of-school-year awards for service to the school or gifts will no doubt surprise and delight them, and encourage others with similar skills to join.

Flipping the Classroom and Library Instruction

Flipped instruction is being discussed and tested in blogs, on Twitter, in educational literature, and in school meetings. Flipping takes instruction that is normally taught within a classroom and makes it independent homework through readings, video lectures or tutorials, or other means. Normal and daily class time is then spent working on an assignment or project that reinforces, enhances, or manipulates the content.

This style should work very well in a library setting when teachers are pinched for time and prefer not to give up class time twice for both media literacy instruction and research. It's tough enough to get classes to the library to perform research under our guidance, but to ask for another bell or class for formal instruction or a game is sometimes impossible. In an attempt to be flexible and to provide instruction and research help, and have students leave with needed information for their project, we can expand our repertoire to include a flip. Why not have our students review the research process through a video tutorial, or peruse the research guide or pathfinder that you created for the assignment before coming to the library. Use or create a video tutorial with your research or orientation game. You can coach, answer questions, suggest better search terms and information sources for a specific need, and solve the teacher's time problem. We know the value of the entire traditional process, and the flipped method may not be our ideal arrangement, but occasionally, it is an alternative and a problem solver, and it will be novel to students. You are likely already providing some flipped instruction if you create and provide video tutorials, virtual help and reference desks, and research pathfinders and guides.

Taking the flip, or electronic help desk, one step further, you can provide an hour or two of online e-mail communication or chat for students on an evening before a research assignment or an individual piece of the assignment is due. For example, if a class's research topic and thesis statement is due on Friday, offer a help session on Tuesday or Wednesday evening. I've offered this service for years and have found students who need it are very grateful and appreciative. If you use e-mail as your communication means, you don't need to be tied to your computer, and you can batch your responses and help to students.

Michael Gorman, author of the blog 21st Century Educational Technology and Learning, is a proponent of the flipped classroom, but he encourages each educator to develop his or her own idea of what that "flip" means. In his July 18, 2012, post, he shares resources that aid in preparation of flipping instruction. Categories of discussion and resources include the following:

- Introduction to the Flip
- Resources To Better Understand Flipping the Classroom
- Higher Level Thinking Skills ... Two Way Interactions. ... Formative Learning ... 21st Century Skills
- Resources To Promote Higher Level Thinking, 21st Century Skills
- Formative Learning in the Flip
- Home Base For Flipping
- Global Communities
- New and Latest

To see more and the resources that fall within each heading, take a look at Gorman's July 2012 post and allow yourself to become curious as you read this introduction to Gorman's post:

> Many educators are beginning to become aware of the growing teaching method referred to as "Flipping The Classroom." Simply put ... the teacher provides videos for homework, while traditional homework is done in class under teacher supervision. Unfortunately this might be just too simplistic of a definition. Possible this is why using the words "simply put" may not be the best practice in explaining anything.
>
> You see, at first this definition does make a lot of sense, and like so many "best practices" I see great value in the idea. In fact, how many parents have sat at the study table with their child only wishing that the teacher was available to explain a math problem? How many students have had to wait until the next day to ask that important question before finishing homework? Before hauling out the video camera

and writing your lesson scripts or perhaps linking to the entire Khan Academy video selection . . . I have several points of reflection.

Yes, I am a proponent of incorporating various multimedia and online learning in a blended environment. In fact . . . there is no doubt that this is the future of education. I say blended because I firmly believe that it is a real teacher that can really make a difference. Blended learning also incorporates some on-line instructional activities. Now, before jumping in the air and doing a full flip, educators must spend some time investigating and contemplating what might work best for their individual situation. Please spend a few moments and allow me to not only provide you with some resources . . . but also as you explore these resources, you may develop some points to ponder. It is my full intention to assist you in coming up with your own definition of the "Flipped Classroom." As you go through the resources below . . . click on the links and immerse yourself. I have tried to find resources that really say it in a way that we can all understand. You may just begin to flip your idea of Flipping.

Your teachers are probably already trying out a flipped classroom method, getting ready to try it, or reading and thinking about it. Help them formulate a path and process by sharing experts' blog posts and resources with them. See Chapter 7 for those experts.

BOOKS

Print, electronic, graphic, and interactive books excite readers.

Speed Dating with Books

I rely on movies, TV, and pop culture to help promote books in my library. I use my Goodreads (http://goodreads.com) account to suggest books to students, teachers, and friends, and I also create plain old and reliable physical book displays with an added pop culture link or connection. Just about anything from pop culture can highlight and bring attention to books. Take speed dating, for example: the term will certainly gain teens' attention, and you can construct the program to fit your school and the appropriateness for your culture and community. Offer students the opportunity to "date" a few books before committing to one. Any brief encounter with a book counts as speed dating. Take a look at a few of the following speed book dating ideas:

1. Create a blog or wiki of recommended and popular book titles that link to a two- to three-minute audio or video book commercial or review.
2. Create your audio or video book commercials with a single teen book reviewer, as a skit with several students, or by utilizing a video creator like Animoto.
3. Use the comic strip format (a few free online sites are available; see Chapter 7 for more information about them).

4. Ask student artists or the art teacher to provide visual representations of a book review. Provide the student or teacher with review guidelines such as characters, intended audience, plot and themes, and so on.
5. Request musical interpretations of a book review but be sure to provide those same book review guidelines (as mentioned in number 4) to them.
6. Create a speed book dating activity for a class of students or a library program. Students participate in pairs with a multiple three-minute speed book dating activity. Pairs sit in chairs across from each other, and a student will try to sell the book that they have already read (and have enjoyed) to the other person. Use a timer, signal when the three-minute intervals are up, and have one line of students move to the left or right to begin again. Students will get to hear what their peers and classmates recommend and have opportunities to recommend their own books. Preparation is key with this activity—it is a live, real-time activity, so students need to think and prepare points of recommendation ahead of time, before they are seated across from someone. Provide, in advance, a template with concepts and evaluation areas that can be reproduced for each student and book that is being recommended. For example, help students understand that character development, target audience, plot, themes, length of text, reading level and difficulty, and tone of the book are important to communicate to their classmates. Have students hold the physical book, or a photo of the book, in their hands and allow time for students to check books out before the class ends. You and the teacher might begin by selling and describing a book to each other to set the tone and provide a real-life example. Ask a student to time you and the teacher.

It's not unusual to have classes that are charged with self-selecting or choosing books from a list within their classes. Students can use help with their selections, and the speed book dating activity is a fun way to incorporate a pop culture trend, provide information about each book, and actively involve all students and their ideas. Students will benefit from revisiting and finding key concepts to "sell" their book, and they will be kinetically involved by physically moving from one chair to the next. The term "speed dating" is what will turn your patrons' heads, creating interest and setting the tone of the activity. The rules and structure of the activity can be anything you can imagine.

Book Displays

I love to create displays that connect books and movies. The most obvious, of course, are movies made from books or books made from movies. It's not beneath me to beg for an older movie poster or display from a movie theatre manager. I've been lucky enough to have a life-size standup poster of a movie character in past years. My husband and children just walk away when they see me eyeing a poster or asking for the theater manager.

Market your eBooks along with your print books. Don't allow those titles to remain invisible just because they don't sit on a shelf in your library. Make a separate display for your eBooks and use posters or flyers with images of the book covers to announce them. Or pull the title's print copy and place pop-up signs or flags in it that announce, "Read Me on a Kindle," "I'm an eBook too," or "Want a copy for your iPad?" Use the pop-up flags for your print books too. Make and place colorful "Pick Me," "Read Me First," and "One of My Favorites" pop-up signs and flags to stick in books in order to pull attention to specific titles. It takes just seconds to type in the phrases, print on color paper, and cut out in a cartoon thought bubble or dialogue cloud. Be sure to leave a long stem to stick into a book.

Use your Photoshop, photo editing skills, or plain old paper, scissors, and glue to display signs of celebrities holding or reading a popular book, and let the stars do the selling for you. Look through magazines for famous people or celebrities holding a book, any book—or something the size of a book and create a tiny book cover of a title that you want to promote to place over the book or item that they are holding. Stick the page into a clear sign holder, and you have a marketing tool with pop culture appeal.

It's not difficult to find connections between books and movies or TV that at first seem unrelated. Try "selling" *Lord of the Flies* side by side with the Hunger Game books, and tell or make signs comparing the books. It's useful to display fiction and popular nonfiction books with topics related to what students are studying in their classes. For example, tell a science teacher or students about a title like *Turn Here, Sweet Corn* by Atina Diffley. The nonfiction book about organic farming reads more like a memoir, and will keep students reading and learning about chemistry and biology as they relate to real life. Go a little further and sell the idea of a science class book project. Show the teacher a list of newer and popular titles that could add interest and related knowledge to the curriculum. Offer to provide booktalks to sell specific titles to students and find the best teasing paragraphs or chapter beginnings to make students want to read more. Ask students for their book suggestions and give students who make good suggestions or give spontaneous mini booktalks of their own the right to choose their books first. Or if you hate doing booktalks, invite a public library teen librarian (hopefully one that you can depend on to dazzle students with engaging booktalks) to bring a collection of topic-related books to your library and to do the booktalks for the students.

All vampire and otherworldly books like Veronica Roth's books *Divergent* and *Insurgent*,will be more likely to be checked out if you position them with the *Twilight* or *Hunger Games* movies and books display. Display some good and dependable nonfiction bibliotherapy items in a display with *The Fault in our Stars* by John Green, *Where Things Come Back* by John Corey Whaley, or any book that deals with illness, loss, and suffering. They might be just what

Pop-up flags to promote books

students need and want after reading these emotional stories to expand their knowledge of a book topic or theme.

Use current events to connect topics and student interests to books. Books that discuss social studies and issues, politics, medical breakthroughs, and local news can all be valuable ways for teens to become more interested in high-value topics. During election campaigns, create a big display of fiction and nonfiction books about elections, government, and politicians. Create a buzz in your library about politics and social awareness. Gather and display campaign posters in a non-partisan way. What you make look important will be perceived as important.

PROGRAMMING IN YOUR LIBRARY

Programs and events transform libraries from arid information warehouses to lively creation places

Celebrities

When creating programming for your library, consider ideas, events, or individuals that aren't typically connected to libraries or education. For example, consider community sports stars or celebrities that might be willing to either appear in person at your school or library to provide a face to any activity or promotion, or to appear by Skype or Facetime; an off-season, major league soccer, football, baseball, or hockey star might be willing to be the celebrity that announces the winners and gives away the prizes for your reading contest or National Library Week contests. Or invite a graduate that has gone on to do great things and whom everyone will recognize or a faculty member's son or daughter who is a famous YA author, important scientist, politician, or media celebrity. To help him or her agree, ask for very little time, schedule at their convenience, and provide exposure. Prepare students so that you'll have the cheering and excited crowds the individual might expect. Take a look at the American Library Association's (ALA) Read Posters for ideas on what wide variety of celebrities might work for you. Every community has individuals who are eager to interact with young people, inspire, promote educational activities, or want to pay forward the good luck and fortune that they've found.

Tweet, Sing, and Be Merry

When I saw the blog postings from the Twitteroke event with karaoke and video games that was offered to conference participants at the International Society for Technology in Education (ISTE) Conference in San Diego in June 2012, I immediately started thinking about how to make that catchy and trendy theme work for students in a school library. What a great idea to connect Twitter, karaoke, and video games to your library, and to create an event that pops with current trends and themes. Here are some ideas to adapt the Twitteroke event for your library:

• Require students to follow the library's Twitter account as their admission into the event.
• Have your Twitter timeline projected on a large screen so that your tweets will be visible to all.

- Send tweets out randomly during the event to keep your participants engaged.
- The first tweet might announce, "Karaoke begins in 10 minutes. Come to the circ desk to sign up."
- A later tweet might state, "The first person to find the book *The Night Circus* by Erin Morgenstern and bring it to me wins a prize."
- Tweet about the location of food and favorite treats.
- Tweet the names of students or teachers who just entered the space.
- Provide karaoke, Wii and other video games, board games, and food.
- Tweet the names of the participants or winners of the karaoke or video games.
- Tweet that a larger prize will be awarded to someone who sings a song that contains lyrics about libraries or librarians.

Yes, there are songs about libraries and librarians. Take a look at these selections: "At the Library" by Green Day; "Swinging London" by the Magnetic Fields; "Fun, Fun, Fun" by the Beach Boys; and "Library Card" by Frank Zappa. Or if students can't find a song about libraries, they can write their own on the spot, which might be even more fun. Any combination of singing, food, prizes, and social media will be too tempting for students to pass up, and what you will gain for your library program is more followers on Twitter, a confirmation that the library offers fun in addition to academics, and that you are approachable.

Fresh ideas can be found anywhere in the world, and it seems that event planners for big library, tech, and education conferences are good—really good—at connecting participants with pop culture. These event planners are masters at finding ways to keep conference-goers busy and happy, and they are very successful at making events from the newest and hottest trends. Even if you are not planning to attend a conference, don't delete any e-mails or announcements about library or tech conferences until you've scanned the conference program and details for ideas about the pop culture being used to create programs, branding, and social events for conference attendees. Especially check out the committee and social events intended for younger (perhaps first-time) attendees and tweak those ideas to create something exciting and new for your patrons.

America's Next Top Poet

During National Poetry Month, collaborate with the creative writing or English teacher and create an open mic event where students can present their original poetry or read from someone else's. Call it Poetry Idol, Bobcats Got Talent, or The Real Poets of Hamilton County (of course, insert your school's mascot and your county). Ask teachers to give extra credit to writing students who participate. Add an edge of competition and appoint a jury or group of judges, depending on your institution's culture, and let everyone have his or her few minutes of fame. Provide an option and separate category for "instant poetry" for participants to create on-the-spot poems based on a word or phrase drawn from a bowl of poetry prompts. If you have a teacher, staff member, alum, or student who has published his or her poems or poetry, appoint him or her as your school's poet laureate and invite him or her to be both honored and to act as the MC for the event. Have categories for both individuals and teams. Take video clips from the event and post them on your website or your digital library display.

Pocket Poetry

During National Poetry Week, or any time that poetry is introduced to your students through individual classes or with an author visit, use an activity like National Poem in your Pocket Day (PIYP) that occurs during National Poetry Month, to highlight poetry.

Various methods of creating poems in pockets activities are encouraged and have been used. There are guidelines but no strict rules from PIYP that you need to follow. Be creative and develop a plan that works for you and your community. Students love receiving things and will pass on their surprise to classmates and friends.

To ensure that students in my school can effortlessly participate, I find, copy, and paste public domain poems from websites or databases—all styles and eras —cut them into small pieces of paper, fold them, and place them in baskets in random locations around the school with a sign that states, "Take a Poem, Read a Poem, Put a Poem in Your Pocket." The simple program takes only the time that I spend finding, printing, cutting, and folding the poems.

Invite Others to Play

Who doesn't like to go outside and play? What librarian doesn't want a change of pace and isn't curious about how others with similar patrons and responsibilities handle day-to-day interactions and roles? Give public YA librarians a chance to see how school libraries and librarians interact with teens. I've invited public YA librarians to my library many times in order to have a fresh face and programming ideas for my students. I have never been turned down. Make a call to your local branch or ask your school librarian colleagues for recommendations. Provide some structure for the librarian: time frame and constraints, theme, ideas that have worked or not worked in the past, technology tools that you can set up and have ready to go, and dates from which to choose. I've even asked for the YA librarian to stay and replay the presentation or activity a couple of times in order to hit all lunch periods or classes.

When inviting others for programs, make sure that you do your marketing and have students or groups that will actually attend. If necessary, do a last minute appeal to students in the cafeteria to come to the library for an activity. Don't assume that when students' stomachs begin to growl they will remember the library's lunchtime program.

Past programs that public YA librarians have created and presented for my students include popular books and movies trivia games, booktalks for edgy books, and a themed trivia game of topics connected to a holiday or season. I've also asked teen librarians to do booktalks directed toward a health class and to bring a collection that can be checked out to them. Public librarians are not frequently asked to work with a captive audience.

Community Read programs are effective and popular in promoting literature as well as discussions about issues and events. They can be created in so many different ways and can include the entire school or community, an entire class or grade, or special groups such as mother and daughter, father and son, grandparents and grandchildren, favorite people and students, and so on. During school, after school, evenings, or weekends can be used in order to fit all community needs. I've been sponsoring faculty and staff book clubs for many years in different schools, and enthusiasm and appreciation is the typical response. Obviously, everyone wants and needs a chance to go out and play.

An enjoyable method of including students, teachers, administrators, and anyone else who happens to be in the building that week in reading and sharing stories is to sponsor a program that stops teachers and students in the middle of their schoolwork, daily for a week, at different times, to read the same book. There is something about having every school member sharing the same unexpected experience that brings a community together. A Spontaneous Burst of Reading, an event I created several years ago, occurred during National Library Week, and my principal agreed to allow spontaneous (at least as it appeared to students) announcements over the PA that invited all students and teachers to stop their normal classroom activity, pick up a book that I'd earlier placed in the classroom, and begin reading. In each classroom, the teacher or a student that the teacher appoints, reads from the book until another PA announcement states that it's time to end the reading and go back to normal classroom activities. It works best to allow at least 20 minutes for the daily activity; it will take some classes longer to begin than others. For easier transition, you can time the ending of the reading with the end of class. An alternative structure is to have one reader over the PA or live broadcast channel read to the entire school. A theatre teacher or student would be a good choice or, if you prefer, you can have your own 20 minutes in the spotlight.

Plan your spontaneous breaks daily and at different times in order to surprise students and not take time away from the same classes. You'll have questions about finishing the book, and you can let everyone know that you have, or can get, copies for them to continue reading when the week is over. If you choose an older title, it should be easy to collect copies from the public library or a half-priced bookstore. Students are excited to read spontaneously, and many students will continue to read the book past the activity. Offer students the opportunity to discuss the book, and set a date and time before they become distracted and move on to something else.

Post It in the Library

Students love contests and opportunities to win something. Reading contests don't need to be your only competitive programming; you can have one-day or one-hour contests that provide instant gratification to students. For example, for the small price of sticky notes, you can create a sticky-note activity and invite students to write their favorite book, magazine, class, or movie on a sticky note and place it on a column or wall of your library. Each contestant can pick up a chocolate kiss, and you can take photos of the wall or column then post them on your webpage, display them in the library or around the school, or tweet or e-mail the photos to teachers and students. Choose a day, week, or lunch period and announce to students and teachers that the sticky-note activity is on. The activity is easy and fast, and it requires no preparation.

Colorful sticky notes are also an inexpensive and easy way to announce new titles, tools, or any information. Place stickies right in the middle of a desktop or laptop computer screen to get students' attention. For example, a bright pink sticky might state, "Check out *The Last Dragonslayer*" or "App of the Week: Grammar Up HD." Any good news can be shared at a moment's notice with the sticky notes, but avoid leaving instructions such as "Be sure to log out" or "No food or drinks." If our hope is to connect with students, those "No" notes will undo what progress we make.

Hunting Permits

Scavenger hunts don't ever seem to get old in schools. The hunts can be disguised as games that don't even resemble a scavenger hunt. This past year, in foreign language classes, QR codes that were used to embed clues and technology took the hunt beyond the content of the class and assignment; at the same time that they were learning about foreign countries and languages, students were learning in a kinetic and enjoyable way about QR codes, applications, and the apps to use them. The activities got students out of their seats and moving around the school. Other students and teachers became curious, and the QR code trend continued all year. Most students today know what QR codes are and how to read them, but you will find a few students and teachers who still haven't interacted with them, and your scavenger hunt will provide them with uses and purposes that might spark a creative idea for classroom assignments and projects. A teacher remarked to me that she now recognizes and understands what that sticker is that I placed on her library card at the beginning of the year. And when the teacher asked her class to pull out their phones (students should download the app if it's not already on their phones) to scan the code, suddenly everyone understood that their library card holds a QR code that provides the library's URL. It's hard to stop the spread of new and useful tools in a school. Perhaps in a classroom this school year, a student will ask a teacher if she can use QR codes to complete a history assignment. She might encode a primary document or photo in her presentation in order to demonstrate to classmates how an entire research project can be embedded into a single slide or page of a document through multiple QR codes. The presentation of her assignment then grows in scope and becomes not only about the subject content, but also about presentation skills, creativity, technology tools, and pop culture.

No More Bored Games

As I mentioned before in Chapter 3, games and gaming are the original social media. Think beyond online and video games to include board games: Chess, Scrabble, Bananagrams, Mad Gab, Trivial Pursuit, and the handheld electronic game Catch Phrase are all educational as well as crowd drawing. Provide them in your library for students to play during free bells or study halls, or organize a game day or evening and invite the entire school, parents, and siblings to participate or to watch. Ask your students before organizing a big gaming event to help with the organizing—let them participate in developing the selection of games, team and individual play, and details. An invitation from students might just draw a few more other students and friends.

BREAKING NEWS AND EVENTS

Librarians are likely to get word of local, national, or global news more quickly than anyone else in the school or institution. Being connected to information resources and social media all day is likely to result in important information being pushed to you as it is occurring. Communicate important news and events to your administration and teachers; when appropriate, stream live coverage. For example, coverage of election results, the presidential inauguration, royal weddings, global news, sports, local announcements, and tech breakthroughs or announcements will offer your patrons up-to-the-minute information. There will be times in the library when this constant information isn't appropriate, but much of the time it will be a welcome addition, and your community will know that your library is the place to go for news coverage. With constant tickers running along the bottom of a screen, it is not always necessary to add audio to follow an event, which will keep distractions to a minimum.

If streaming live news and events won't work in your library, you should still constantly share current headline news and events through displays, posters, and props. Tie the events and information into curriculum and assignments that you know your students are studying and working on. For example, for science classes that are studying astronomy or weather, create a plan to observe

Astronomy Day in October. Celebrate important celestial occurrences by finding and printing images of past events and using them as posters or signage; create displays of binoculars and star charts, and a map of the night sky. Create a dynamic section of your display to announce that night's moon phase, weather forecast, and any other related information. Pull books from your shelves that provide more scientifically related information, biographies or memoirs of astronomers, and fiction that uses astronomy as a theme.

Want to celebrate the Northern Lights, but you live in Florida? Display a video of the Northern Lights and provide information about where and how they can be experienced and viewed by the human eye. Add maps and viewing forecasts of the closest viewing location to your city and the farthest city away from you, and add mileage, accessibility, and differences between the closest and farthest cities.

TECHNOLOGY SHOW AND TELL

Have a technology show-and-tell session in the library. Use all the tech tools, devices, and gadgets that you can beg and borrow or that you already own. Ask for volunteers to bring a tool to demonstrate or request those who have experience and knowledge about specific devices to say a few words about them. Or don't do a presentation at all and just provide signage with a description of each one and offer hands-on time for everyone to play with them.

With a slightly different focus, offer a Latest and Greatest Tech News session that doesn't involve handheld tools, but tech related information that impacts both professional and personal lives. Have a wiki, website, research pathfinder, or guide loaded with links to news, information, explanations and descriptions, videos, blogs, and websites that discuss and present information about new technology topics or trends. Do a quick overview and explanation of what you've provided along with how you've organized and categorized what they are likely to discover. Then (quickly) set them free to explore and follow the links. Participants will likely share and discuss findings with each other, and find a tool or topic to use in the classroom. Topics might include news about the release of the free Microsoft Office 365 for education, the newest releases or expectations for electric cars, how police surveillance of U.S. mobile phones has skyrocketed, comparison of the newest smart phones and tablets, or contrasting features of streamed movie sites such as Netflix and Hulu. Teachers rarely get free time and opportunities to peruse the latest information, and it's a bonus that they are exploring information and topics that you have vetted and selected. It's likely that your participants will leave knowing that the library is the place to go for the latest news about technology.

Obviously, you can follow blogs, Twitter, Facebook, journals, and websites to find out what programming ideas exist, but also consider looking at local, national, and global technology and library conference schedules, programs, and sessions to find the newest and best programming ideas. Sessions and workshops that are being offered currently or in the near future are likely to cover popular best practices that have been utilized with success. Sometimes a description of a session or program will be all you need to run with an idea or to spark a new idea of your own that will create something unique for your students and community.

HOLIDAYS AND CELEBRATIONS

Mandarin Chinese–language classes in high school are steadily increasing across the United States. It's likely that your school already offers at least one level of the language, that it will soon, or that it is pointing students to local or online programs. Support global awareness and your students' interest in China and Chinese language by creating displays and visual materials for everyone to see when they visit the library.

2013 is the Year of the Snake. Inexpensively, you can celebrate Chinese New Year with lanterns, dragons, snakes, fortune cookies, chopsticks, and other related items. Give away fortune cookies to each person who checks out a book that has something (anything) to do with China. Provide signage that defines symbols, words, and traditions. Create a poster of the Chinese zodiac snake with an explanation of what that means, and create smaller posters of all of the zodiac signs so that everyone will be able to locate their personal sign and description.

It is an endless pleasure in a school setting to celebrate, teach, and recognize cultures from around the world. Today's world is small and growing smaller through technology and industry, and the abundance of resources and information offers so much material from which to pull ideas and create awareness. Make those connections to other cultures as frequently as possible and extend lessons, projects, and interest from the classroom right down the hall or stairway into your library.

NEW TRENDS IN LIBRARIES

Innovative activities, repurposed space, and increased patron interaction are helping to keep libraries relevant in today's fast-paced world.

Makerspaces

A phenomenon that is popping up in communities all over the world is called makerspaces. The terms "hackerspaces" and "backlabs" as well as a number of other terms are sometimes used interchangeably with the word "makerspaces," but the concept is the same. Makerspaces are developed by communities of individuals that create a physical gathering space that serves as a center of creativity, brainstorming, and collaboration. Makerspaces were originally, and many still are, independent facilities unrelated to library institutions. HIVE13, a makerspace in Cincinnati, is a facility and brainchild of a group who describes their space as:

> Hive13 aims to create a place where a diverse community of makers can collaborate and pursue creative projects. Hive13 promotes science & technology education, open source values, and skill sharing amongst its members and the community. (July 23, 2012)

Some cutting-edge libraries are making the makerspaces concept into a physical and readily available facility for patron use. In addition to a science and technology focus, which was common in makerspaces' earliest days, other partnerships between libraries and art and cultural institutions are being pursued. For example, the website and blog Library as Incubator (http://www.libraryasincubatorproject.org/), created in the fall of 2011 by three librarians —Laura Damon-Moore, Erinn Batykefer, and Christina Endres—aids collaborations among all types of artists (visual, performance, writers) and educational institutions. As in a makerspace tradition, physical space and resources are offered to individuals and groups. The mission of the website, clearly indicates a proactive approach to rethinking and transforming library space:

> The mission of the Library as Incubator Project is to promote and facilitate creative collaboration between libraries and artists of all types, and to advocate for libraries as incubators of the arts. We serve this mission both through the Library as Incubator Project website and through other offline projects.
>
> On our website we:
>
> - Feature artists, writers, performers and libraries who exemplify the "library as incubator" idea.
> - Highlight physical and digital collections and resources that may be of particular use to artists and writers.
> - Provide ideas for art education opportunities in libraries with our program kit collection and practical how-to's for artists and librarians.

An example of a successful project that has resulted from initiatives promoted by Library as Incubator is a digital literacy project at the Carnegie Library. The project resulted in teen-produced videos created through the Labs QuickFlix workshops.

School libraries and librarians have a long history of providing workshops for teens that result in videos, homemade books, poetry performances, and more. Is the term just another facet of learning to add to our school library repertoire? We already share the goals of collaboration, providing tools and resources, learning, teaching, and creation.

Develop a plan and tools, and perhaps recruit a teacher from a specific subject area to create a makerspaces site in your school or library. Market your makerspaces setting to provide the platform for teens and other patrons to go beyond the library's traditional intellectual property resource sharing and knowledge, to add a physical space that promotes the hands-on skills and implementation of what our students are studying and learning in art, science, and technology classes in our schools.

In her June 28, 2012, post titled "Makerspaces, Participatory Learning, and Libraries," Buffy Hamilton, author of the blog the Unquiet Librarian (http://theunquietlibrarian.wordpress.com), explains the concept of makerspaces and how they offer opportunities to develop participatory learning experiences for students. In addition, Hamilton provides methods for readers to explore makerspaces further. Allow the following post to ignite your curiosity and creativity, visit her resources, and consider how you might make this learning opportunity work for your students:

The concept of libraries as makerspaces first hit my radar last November when I read about the Fayetteville Free Library's FabLab (http://infospace.ischool.syr.edu/2011/12/01/a-makerspace-takes-over-a-local-library/). As I began hearing more buzz about libraries and makerspaces the first few months of this year, I decided that learning more about this concept and exploring how I might apply the elements of makerspaces to my library program would be a personal learning project for the summer.

So what is a makerspace? Makerspace defines it as:

"Modeled after hackerspaces, a makerspace is a place where young people have an opportunity to explore their own interests, learn to use tools and materials, and develop creative projects. It could be embedded inside an existing organization or standalone on its own. It could be a simple room in a building or an outbuilding that's closer to a shed. The key is that it can adapt to a wide variety of uses and can be shaped by educational purposes as well as the students' creative goals."

The Library as Incubator Project (http://www.libraryasincubatorproject.org/) describes makespaces as:

"Makerspaces are collaborative learning environments where people come together to share materials and learn new skills . . . makerspaces are not necessarily born out of a specific set of materials or spaces, but rather a mindset of community partnership, collaboration, and creation."

In late spring, I was even more intrigued by the concept as my friends and colleague Kristin Fontichiaro began sharing some her thoughts on makerspaces and the possibilities for school libraries. While immersing myself into researching makerspaces last week, I discovered friend and fellow librarian Heather Braum (http://www.twitter.com/hbraum) is also fascinated by the possibilities, and she shared her current list of resources with me including photos and video from her visit this past weekend to the Kansas City Maker Faire. You can learn more about Heather's Maker Faire experience in her new blog post here http://www.heatherbraum.info/libraries/maker-faire-kc-2012/.

While I am having fun soaking up ideas and brainstorming ways we could cultivate makerspaces in The Unquiet Library, I can't help but notice that makerspaces provide opportunities for participatory learning. As regular readers of the blog know, participatory learning (http://playnml.wikispaces.com/PLAY!+Framework) is the guiding framework for my library program and services. Project New Media Literacies (http://henryjenkins.org/2011/05/shall_we_play_part_two.html) identifies these principles of participatory learning:

- Heightened motivation and new forms of engagement through meaningful play and experimentation
- Learning that feels relevant to students' identities and interests
- Opportunities for creating using a variety of media, tools, and practices.
- Co-configured expertise where educators and students pool their skills and knowledge and share in the tasks of teaching and learning
- An integrated system of learning where connections between home, school, community and world are enabled and encouraged

I believe that makerspaces can provide students AND teachers opportunities to exercise these elements of participatory learning and to form what James Gee calls affinity spaces (http://en.wikipedia.org/wiki/Affinity_space), communities formed around passions and shared interests. Tinkering, collaborative learning, play, conversations for learning, intergenerational learning, experimentation, inquiry, the act of creation, and problem solving—these are just some of the qualities that can happen in makerspaces and encourage participatory learning.

The Unquiet Library blog provides many resources about makespaces as well as other topics that promote participatory learning and discover. And check out Chapter 7 for more contact information for Buffy Hamilton.

TOMORROW'S LIBRARIAN LIVING ON THE LEADING EDGE TODAY

It is a formidable—or at least threatening—idea to plan to immediately change and recharge our library programs. Most librarians who work in schools or in public libraries with teens have so many directions and responsibilities to fill the days, and sometimes evenings, that one more distraction might lead to that infamous breaking point. But to create lasting change for our students, we need to at least have an understanding of what is new and shiny in the library world. Who best can tell us what is heading our way, or already in our path, than a current library school student preparing to leap into the library world.

Mia Breitkopf, a former high school teacher and current library school student at the iSchool at Syracuse University is an example of the next crop of librarians who are digital natives and for whom makerspaces and emerging technologies hold no mystique or trepidation. To Mia, blogging, Twitter, and concepts like makerspaces are just everyday life. Mia blogs as naturally as most of us breathe, and her December 1, 2011, post on the University of Syracuse's blog, Infospace (http://infospace.ischool.syr.edu/2011/12/01/a-makerspace-takes-over-a-local-library/) about makerspaces taking over a library space caught my attention. For one, the term "makerspace" was relatively new to me, and this library student's confidence and knowledge about the newest trends made me want to know more about her and other emerging librarians. Meet Mia and hear about her library school education and the voice of tomorrow's librarian.

TOMORROW'S LIBRARIAN READY TO LEAD THE WAY

I was feeling a bit out of my element. It was week one of library school, and I'd already been required to set up a personal blog and join Twitter. My professors were actually suggesting I tweet during class! I realize now that they were already training us to be librarians. It was a study in community development. As I got to know them in person, my colleagues' Twitter feeds and our class hashtags soon became an integral part of my curriculum, as we discussed and shared what we were writing and reading, online and in the classroom. I started blogging for my school, and people outside my immediate community started to read and comment on my thoughts. By week five I was having conversations online with people around the country.

Part of a fresh generation of librarians

We 21st century library and information science students embrace long-held tenets of librarianship, like preservation of access, civil liberties, and intellectual freedom. But we are a new breed. We're tech-savvy, ambitious, socially conscious information professionals. We know we've got to learn quickly and stay flexible. We hold Google Hangout team meetings, use Dropbox and Evernote to co-write project plans, and host webinars. We're ready to be sent out to work in a library building or classroom—or, better yet, in the community park, out on the sidewalks, or in city hall.

Doom-and-gloom reports about the future of libraries haven't deterred practical, bright, and passionate people from enrolling in LIS degree programs. In fact, negative press about librarianship has lit a fire under me, and my fellow students. We're on a mission to support the foundations of librarianship while moving the field into the future. Questions like "Are libraries becoming obsolete?" are a waste of time for us. We're more apt to ask, "How will we improve and empower our communities?"

BIOGRAPHY: MIA BREITKOPF

Mia will graduate in the spring of 2013 with her master's degree in library and information science from Syracuse University. In 2011, she moved to Syracuse with her husband to study librarianship after seven years in Philadelphia, PA, where she taught public school general music and worked for The Pew Center for Arts & Heritage, an arts and culture grantmaker. Mia has a bachelor's degree in music education from the Crane School of Music at The State University of New York at Potsdam.

5

Connect to Today's Teens through Media and Technology Tools

THE DEVICE OF THE MOMENT

Ten years ago, it was a choice of laptops, desktop computers, Blackberry cell phones, and Palm Pilots. Cutting-edge schools had classroom carts, computer labs, and were migrating, or at least considering, to a one-to-one environment.

No matter what computer environment a school chose 10 years ago, most are now questioning, rethinking, undoing, and planning anew in order to participate in the popularity and success of handheld devices.

iPads, Nooks, Kindles, smart phones with Android or Apple technology, and iTouches are seen in almost every pocket, purse, backpack, or bag. It's no longer a game for the young or early adopters—fathers, mothers, grandparents, young siblings, and both techies and nontechies are likely to own one or more of these devices.

BYOD

Schools are counting on the iPad, Nook, Kindle, and other smart devices to bring visual and interactive content to classrooms. In addition to the classroom content, personal devices are our connection and our students' connection to our digital and social worlds. It is odd that in many schools that tout technology integration, students enter a "no access" zone when they walk through the school doors in the morning. They don't have access to the school's network with their own devices, and they are not permitted use of their personal devices during the school day. That seems counterproductive. Much classroom time focuses on helping students learn skills to manage their time, schedules, and calendars; take notes; and keep track of homework assignments and documents. The personal devices that they bring with them hold, or can hold, the important information that they, and we, need at a moment's notice—calendars, schedules, notes, tasks, documents, and contacts that are requisite to work and school. There are many apps designed specifically for managing these essential tasks and information that can become invaluable tools for students' educational experience.

A bring your own device (BYOD) philosophy is likely to satisfy almost every educational objective that a school might have. It teaches responsibility and tech agility, integrates technology into the classroom, makes learning relevant and meaningful, provides student-centered learning, provides tools to reach every type of learner, and much more. However, most would agree that the management, control, and learning curve for teachers, technology staff, and administrators might be very steep. Many questions arise when students bring devices into a school. For example, who are students communicating with in the bathroom or hall? What distractions are being added to all the other school distractions? How can teachers know that a student is on task? How can we prevent students from texting answers or information to each other during tests and quizzes? Does the gap widen between those students with devices and those without? Does it make sense to have every school computer and device locked tight with security measures but the devices that student bring in the door to be wide open and unfiltered? There are so many other reasons to develop— and not to develop—a BYOD program that it comes down to making the best choice for each individual school setting. If your school isn't ready or planning to adopt a BYOD program, and if you already have a one-to-one program or carts full of fun devices, there are still opportunities to have students experience more than a single device. Consider the options presented later in this section in the section titled "Which Device?"

Some forward-thinking schools understand how important it is to integrate the use of devices and their features into everyday lives, and these schools offer students the opportunity to bring your own device, especially since most teens and preteens already own at least one of the most popular devices. Some schools are using a different approach and providing either a school-chosen device to every incoming class or to every enrolled student, or carts and classroom sets or devices. The good news is that mobile devices are getting into the hands of students. However, some methods seem better suited to today's devices than others. Mobile tools are developed, and work best, as personal devices. They are not as ideal in a classroom cart or lab situation. For example, the personal features and accounts related to Twitter, Pinterest, Facebook, note-taking and time management tools, individual preferences of reading apps, and the opportunity to carry one's entire eBook and digital document library is lost when devices are not personally owned and maintained. And the apps that create and store completed or in-progress projects are difficult to manage with multiple users. However, features such as subject-related apps and resources, high-resolution video for viewing, and many more features can be beneficial when the device is only borrowed for a class. In the end, no matter what a school's policies are regarding devices and the school's network, imperfect and temporary access is better than no access at all.

In his March 10, 2012, post "BYOD and the Library," Doug Johnson, author of the Blue Skunk Blog, describes the importance of school libraries embracing the BYOD approach. He lists the goals of his school's BYOD program:

- To increase motivation and engagement in the classroom
- To help provide access to a wide variety of resources that support differentiated instruction efforts
- To help provide increased student access to school provided eBooks, e-textbooks, and Moodle units
- To provide the means for online collaborative work in the classroom
- To develop workable rules and standards for classroom teachers to help manage student-owned technologies

But Johnson also warns of issues to consider before implementing a BYOD program:

So what does this have to do with libraries? These are some things all librarians should be asking themselves if their schools are figuring out means of giving al students continuous access to online resources, whether student or school owned.

- Do my library rules and policies help students take advantage of their mobile computing device?
- Can students and staff get knowledgeable support from my library staff when they have technical problems?
- Am I selecting library resources with mobile computing devices in mind?
- In my role as instructional leader, am I using best practices that take advantage of a ubiquitous technology environment—and helping my teachers do so as well?
- Do I exemplify a learner who takes advantage of having continuous access to my PLN and to the world's information?

Is you school one-to-one or BYOD? If so, how are you as a librarian supporting this effort?

If we don't figure this out, we may not be BYOD, but DOA.

Whether your school promotes the BYOD program or is a one-to-one school, or you put devices into your students' hands with carts, classroom sets, or library loaners, continue to urge your school to adopt policies that best prepare students for a quickly changing and mobile world. Teens, inside and outside of school, need to maintain and further develop their tech agility and to be able to tinker and test the limits and features of today's newest technology in order to excel, not just survive, in tomorrow's educational arena and workplace.

Current and constantly changing tech advancements place a huge responsibility on schools to educate and develop this generation's tech skills and abilities. With regular and continuous access to these new and newer mobile tools, students will be able to easily transfer their knowledge to the next great device and learning situation. The devices are more than toys. When using tech tools and mobile devices, teaching and learning should remain focused on content, but the device and entertainment value of the tool is very important in schools. Today's students' future challenges and real-world successes are dependent on how they learn and use today's tools, and these technology devices allow the interaction that makes learning enjoyable and engaging for students.

WHICH DEVICE IS RIGHT?

Handheld devices can be so many things—tablets, smart phones, iPods, gaming devices, eBook readers, and more. Some serve multiple purposes and satisfy many needs. Some are big, some are small, and most have touch and color screens.

No matter if your school is a one-to-one environment with laptops or tablets, if you have carts or labs that provide devices, or if you are participating in a BYOD program, or if you have a hybrid of methods, you surely have some experience with a device or two. However, look for ways to give your students experience with other devices. No single laptop, tablet, or smart phone does it all for everyone, and the more experience students acquire with and between multiple devices, the more tech agility they will develop. The ultimate result of tech agility is lifelong skills that ensure an easy and confident transition to the next newest tech tool and beyond.

iPads and other tablets are clearly the leaders in providing the widest variety and readily available tools for most users in a single device. Tomorrow's device might not resemble today's tablet at all. Almost daily we see news reports of concept devices with bendable screens or devices, computerized lenses to wear as eye glasses that display our computer information, monitors or billboards that provide instantaneous information that has been programmed for our personal consumer interests, and a number of 3D tools that seem to lift information off the flat computer screen. Most of these tools are still in the concept stage, but what is here today are information pop-ups and ads tailored to recent search history that appear on the top, side, and bottom of the browser to display brands, products, and items designed to tempt the viewer. The magical and sometimes scary way these products target and compete for the viewer's attention offers a glimpse into the marketing approaches of tomorrow. Marry those approaches with the concept tools mentioned earlier, and it is likely that tomorrow's students will need even more sophisticated media literacy skills and knowledge to navigate the ubiquitous information maze.

While reading and watching ads for today's most popular devices, it appears that consumers make their choices based on size, weight, camera and video features, and screen resolution. And most technology news and blogs claim that iPad outsells all other tablets primarily due to the better availability and quality of apps for iPads. For example, with iPads, library users can choose to read iBooks through Apple's iBook reader, or they can choose many other eBook apps like the Amazon Kindle app, Ebook.com's eBook reader, and others. These apps not only allow readers to access the books chosen, but the apps provide options and direct links to bookstores and libraries so that the viewer can find eBooks. Who knows if allowing competitors' apps on the iPad will continue—competitors are hungry for tablet users to choose their own devices and perhaps by limiting apps that are compatible with the iPad, their own tablets will sell better. For example, all over the news in early August 2012 was the announcement that Google, YouTube's parent company, no longer preloads the very popular built-in YouTube app on the iPad, iPhone, and iPod Touch. There appears to be little impact for IOS users because the app is freely available to download on any IOS device. At this point, the Apple devices are holding their own without much injury from the offensive moves to lessen Apple's control of the market.

In a perfect world, a single eBook reader would read any digital text regardless of what publisher or platform developed it, but in today's world of proprietary rights and digital rights management (DRM) specific to each publisher, vendor, and platform, those issues are controlling our choices. The problem for now is solved, although somewhat clunky, by adding as many apps to our tablets as we need, or as many devices as we can afford or that makes sense to purchase, in order to allow us to choose from different price points and read and offer our patrons books from our current and past eBook collections, as well as from today's public libraries, Project Gutenberg, Amazon, Apple, Barnes and Noble, and Google.

In the school library, we attempt (as we always have) to satisfy individual patrons' needs and wants, for whatever tools they carry in their backpack or briefcase. Today, if a student or teacher has a readily available laptop, tablet, or iPhone and needs a book that you have loaded and available in your Kindle loaning library, you have a couple of choices: pop out and offer the library's Kindle reader to the patron with ready-to-go downloaded titles or offer to loan the title to him or her through your library and his or her Kindle app for PC, Mac, iPad, iPhone, BlackBerry, or Android devices. Kindle books, depending on the publisher, can be loaned once to another user with a different account (however, the book will not be available to the owner during the loan period). For example, our library can loan the Kindle book *Bridge of Sighs* by Richard Russo that we have purchased through our Amazon account to a patron for his or her own device one time, or we can share *Bridge of Sighs* up to six times between devices that are registered to our library. Another option is to see if the title is available through a local public library and help the patron download the title immediately to his or her device. In addition, the on-demand purchasing is attractive as it allows the library to buy a title to fill an immediate need when the need presents itself.

Should school libraries wait and see before taking the eBook reader or tablet plunge? I don't think so. There will never be an end to the waiting and seeing; newer and different devices and eBook issues will continue to be added to the current issues. The clear advantage is in taking the plunge now. If you have committed to transforming your library to satisfy the needs of today's learners, then the need exists today even if the decision to purchase them today is still muddy.

Maybe this comparison will help with the decision. No doubt you eagerly (or reluctantly) added digital cameras and video cameras to your collection years ago. Consider the price of those devices and the benefit they provide along with the need they satisfy. And compare the price of those cameras with the price of a Kindle reader or tablet. Your investment will not be much greater than for one of those cameras or the software you purchased in addition to the devices so that students could edit video and create movies. If you are still not convinced, consider that the price of an eBook device is comparable to the cost of a few print monographs that are single titles serving single users one at a time.

How do small libraries decide which book readers to purchase? Of course, it's an individual decision, but the wisest decision might be to offer what isn't already available to your patrons. If that sounds counterintuitive, consider that your patrons are not going to ask you for something that they already have or have access to. What your patrons will want is that which they don't have or that which is harder to find. For example, if your school provides iPads to students, acquire and offer Kindle or Nook readers that are loaded with requested titles. Consider promoting audio books in your school and build a collection of PlayAway audio devices or CD audio books, or find free audio book downloads from a public domain website. Provide devices for students to read the downloaded books by purchasing and loaning out MP3 players or iPods for mobile use. Although the purchase of MP3 players and iPods might seem to be redundant because students can use (and most already own) smart phones, laptops, or another type of computer, consider that those tablets, laptops, and smart phones are not very practical for reading on the move. Laptops are heavy, most tablets won't fit in a pocket, and smart phones have limited battery life with likely interruptions by phone calls, messaging, and alerts. And the trend is to satisfy the constant movement and mobility that describe our students' lives as well as our own. Consumers, especially students and teens, want access wherever, whenever, and however they go.

New and improved apps are rolling out faster than I can type this sentence, and most apps satisfy a user's needs inexpensively and conveniently. The education world is just beginning to feel the impact of what tools like tablets and apps can do. Although a discussion of apps clearly fits into a dialogue of devices, technology, and media, they deserve a chapter of their own because of their popularity and how many there are to recommend and describe. For recommendations of the apps I think are essential, fun, or you should have some knowledge about, see Chapter 6.

THE CLOUD

As discussed in prior chapters, the iPad, along with all of the other favorite tablets and handheld devices, are changing how we interact with information. Remember back to five years ago, or even just last year, when you would see people wearing their USB drives around their neck all day long or carrying them on a keychain? Remember worrying about whether you backed up your documents and files before you left for the day or on vacation? Wasn't that just yesterday? We are now free to worry about other things. For instance, I now worry about whether I uploaded the newest version of my document to every cloud storage device I use. I can't think of another recent behind-the-scenes development that has made such a difference in our lives. The cloud doesn't get the press that devices do—it isn't sparkly like the iPad, Kindle Fire, or Nook; it's not visible on the street or at coffee shops; and we don't brag to our families and friends about using the cloud. But it makes all of these mobile instruments, and all of our computers and laptops at school and work, be managed easily and well.

Because of the cloud, mobile devices are small and light. These low weights are possible because the devices don't need to provide much storage. All of our information and many of the programs that we used and that lived on our laptops or other computers are now in the cloud. We no longer have the same worries about losing or breaking our tablets, phones, or iPads. Compared to the high cost of a laptop or desktop computer, they are much less expensive, and all of the data and information can be retrieved for the replacement device from the cloud. Through the cloud, we can sync and share effortlessly among devices, and with a single update to our personal or class calendar we can share items with our students or to our family's shared calendar.

Who, What, Where Is That Cloud?

There is a good chance that you are already using the cloud but just haven't recognized that it is the cloud you've been using for creating online calendars or Google Docs in Google Drive and using online databases, iTunes, Dropbox, Evernote, Amazon's Cloud Storage, Apple's iCloud, SkyDrive, Box, Flicker, or an online app or eBook reader. If you've used any of these items or devices, you already have your head and your files in the clouds. Some of these cloud tools are only for storing files, and others are for producing, editing, and storing. Some are accessed anywhere and through numerous types of devices, and some work from a downloaded client. iTunes is an example of a downloaded client that requires software to be enabled on a device; however, the actual storage of your information occurs in the cloud. Google—through Google Drive (Google Docs)—has been providing cloud services for a decade or more and has led the way for free production tools and file conversion services, as well as free storage for existing documents, presentations, spreadsheets, and photos.

Other big technology companies are aggressively trying to grab some of the cloud services market with their own sites. Microsoft surprised the learning community at the ISTE Conference in June 2012 with the announcement that the cloud service Office 365—which includes e-mails, calendars, video chat, Microsoft Office productivity tools, storage, and more—is now being offered to educational institutions for free. As the cloud grows larger and technology companies and players invest more of their resources in the cloud, it seems obvious that the cloud is going to remain in our technology environment.

All of the cloud services mentioned previously offer free storage of limited amounts of space, and they all offer additional storage for fairly low costs.

Cloud storage provides much more to users than the actual storage space. The cloud gives us peace of mind. I can, as well as teachers and students, access my cloud information and accounts anywhere without worrying about operating systems, updated or outdated programs, or a specific computer or device. Students and teachers no longer need to worry about the time involved and the reliability of bringing their presentations into the classroom, setting them up, and keeping their fingers crossed that they will work on and with a specific device. Students and teachers can have their presentations set up in as little time as it takes to log in and open a file. None of us needs to worry any more about losing files or the risk of having every digital photo or document lost forever on a crashed hard drive. All we need is the web, a web browser, and a username and password.

Cloud storage also solves the issue of future accessibility to our information. There is nothing device-driven or mechanical that will become outdated and limit access to our personal information at some future time. As file formats change or evolve, so will the ability and opportunity to convert them. And if we lose a laptop, iPad, or iPhone, we can find comfort knowing that only the device has been lost and not the documents, photos, contacts, and other content. But don't forget that the storage is only as up-to-date as the user makes it. If the latest version of your novel's manuscript hasn't been uploaded, it won't

Table 5.1

Comparison of Cloud Storage Services

Cloud Storage Device	Amount of Free Space/ Gigabytes (G)	Device or Operating System
iCloud	5 G	iOS and Macs
SkyDrive	7 G	Windows
Dropbox	2 G	All devices with a web browser and requires a downloadable app
Box	5 G	All devices with a web browser
Sugarsync	5 G	All devices with a web browser
JustCloud	Unlimited	All devices with a web browser
Google	5 G	All devices with a web browser
Amazon Cloud Drive	5 G	All devices compatible with Flash

magically appear up-to-date in your cloud storage—operator error still remains the number one reason for technology failures.

See Table 5.1 for a comparison of some popular cloud services that offer some free storage.

eBooks

Everyone is a book lover. Not everyone is an eBook lover. A lot of us are eBook likers and users, but we can't fall in love yet because of the amount of confusion and complication associated with digital books. As an eBook early adopter and user (I read digital text on a Palm Pilot in the 1990s), I still get overwhelmed and frustrated with the process and steps associated with each different book app, reading device, vendor platform, publisher, and options for getting that book to my electronic bookshelf. As a school librarian and the decision maker about what, where, and how to purchase eBooks for my patrons, I approach every new purchase cautiously, as I do every new publisher, vendor, and system. The cost, access, and licensing problems involved with digital books are constant concerns. Questions that float through my head late at night include:

- Is the eBook shelf or website provided by a specific vendor or publisher the best way for our patrons to find and read titles?
- How easily will our students and patrons navigate through and across multiple eBook shelves and websites from multiple vendors?
- Is it better to teach students to search for nonfiction eBook titles through a database topic search, along with articles, reference, and news?
- Should we simply add eBook records to our catalogs in order to stress that eBooks are still books, as we know them, with a different delivery method?

- Or should we stress that eBooks with interactive features are a new breed of books and different than those books that we've always known?
- Is it possible to teach all methods and have patrons choose what works best for them personally? Or will that confuse our patrons (further)?
- Is it logical to pay more for the simultaneous users option even if there's only a slight chance that the specific title will need the option?

J. K. Rowling's Pottermore books are currently demonstrating that eBooks can be developed across platforms to use in any device. I'm hoping that Harry Potter's magic will once again come to the rescue and that our students will eventually be able to read any eBook on any eBook reader or device. For more flexibility and choices, wouldn't most consumers and librarians be willing to pay higher costs for eBooks?

While we leave Rowling and Harry Potter to lead the way for the practical cross-platform development of eBooks, we might consider another option for providing eBooks to our patrons. Brain Hive—a very user-friendly new eBook program—has rolled out a low-cost rental option for eBooks in schools and school libraries. Brain Hive (http://www.BrainHive.com/) is a pay-as-you-go library of eBooks for K-12 schools with free registration for school librarians and principals. Books are loaned for $1 per eBook, institutions have the option to purchase popular books, and institutions can cancel subscriptions at any time. Brain Hive has over 3,000 books, but a limited collection of a just over 100 titles show up when searching only the high school collection. Luckily, plans to grow the collection are underway. Brain Hive's eBook collection is a combination of both fiction and nonfiction titles that come from notable publishers such as Lerner Publishing, Open Road Integrated Media, Random House Children's Books, and more. Ten free loans are provided with new registrations so that users can give Brain Hive a try before investing their own money. The Book Club feature of Brain Hive is a good way to try out the program, as titles can be borrowed by simultaneous users and renewed according to the profile you create for your library and school. In addition, as the administrator, you can set a budget limit and choose monthly, quarterly, or annual budget durations to help keep track of expenditures. More good news about Brain Hive includes the news that an iPad app is available, and the eBooks allow readers to take notes and highlight in the eBooks.

In order to keep up with the ongoing eBook discussion and breaking news about issues concerning eBooks, most library eyes are on eBook expert Sue Polanka, author of the blog No Shelf Required (http://www.libraries.wright .edu/noshelfrequired). Polanka, who makes the complicated seem a bit more manageable through any one of her books, posts, articles, and interviews, makes me feel better about my ability to manage digital formats.

Although Polanka is an academic librarian (she is head of reference/instruction at the Wright State University Libraries in Dayton, Ohio), her approach and scope reach all libraries and levels. Categories that I frequently visit through her blog to discover recent news about eBooks include Accessibility, Articles of Interest, Audio Books, Collection Development, DRM, Ebook Readers, Text-books, Lending Readers, Mobile Devices, and School Libraries.

An example of invaluable information provided through No Shelf Required is the July 5, 2012, post that describes a timely discussion of eBook issues and concerns that took place in the program The E-Elephant in the Room at the 2012 American Library Association's (ALA) annual conference. Polanka was part of the mixed academic and public libraries panel, and the post brings attention to the common issues and concerns surrounding eBooks including:

- Examining E-books from a business model perspective with different possibilities.
- Making decisions about specific software, interfaces, DRM, and establishing a relationship with vendors.
- Developing long-term solutions for collection development.
- Considering a just-in-time approach to purchasing content.
- Developing a hybrid of the two methods above.
- Pursuing consortia purchases for eBooks in order to share access across the consortia, unlimited simultaneous use, and unlimited lifetime use.
- Understanding challenges associated with the differences in various vendors' interfaces, DRM restrictions, number of users, and business models.
- Finding commonalities and solutions with the background and experiences associated with the state of Ohio's OhioLink consortia with regard to eBooks.

In addition, Polanka's post includes discussion points from other eBook experts, including topics such as budgeting for eBooks, evaluating and measuring eBook impact and use, and self-publishing issues. For the complete July 5, 2012, post, go to http://www.libraries.wright.edu/noshelfrequired/2012/07/05/ala-program-summary-e-elephant-in-the-room/.

Librarians and educators benefit greatly from bloggers who participate in these important discussions and report the events to us through their blogs and other social media. We have access to and knowledge of topics that eBook leaders and experts are discussing without needing to be present in real time.

If eBooks are something that you haven't integrated into your library yet or something that you are afraid to imagine, it's time to take charge right now. It's a great time to face eBooks and to begin making decisions about how they will benefit your students, teachers, and library program. People like Sue Polanka have done the hard research and work for us, and their blog posts, articles and books, and presentations have vetted the eBook process and its complications. Follow the experts, read, listen, and plan.

LIBRARY CATALOGS

The library catalog is likely to be the most basic and consistent technology across all libraries, small or large, school or public, rural or urban. Some small libraries are still waiting to upgrade to an electronic library catalog, but for the most part, we have all experienced the efficiency and comfort that electronic catalogs provide to our patrons and us. It's the single technology that is nonnegotiable and one that requires much research and reflection when we need to switch or upgrade to a new management system. It's not easy to decide whether to remain a solo site with our own self-contained library management system or to join a network in the big world beyond our building or school. There are advantages and disadvantages for both decisions—it is not a decision to make without a lot of research and thought.

Who would think that discussion of the catalog would fit into a book about recharging and reinventing library programs, and a chapter specifically about media and technology? Catalogs are no longer just utilities for organizing and storing our libraries' resources. Catalogs are worth discussing because of the way in which catalog features and tools are improving and increasing almost daily, and because of the abundance of information and services that they provide to our patrons. Catalogs have vastly expanded e-content with book cover images, summaries, tables of contents, book reviews, and direct access to other libraries in your system, consortium, city, or region.

This advancement in catalog development is both exciting and worrisome. We can't imagine a world without fast and seamless electronic copy cataloging, and we appreciate seeing students recognize familiar book covers, read reviews, and scan tables of contents through the catalog, but we also worry that every new feature is likely to cost more money now and in the future. However, in the end, because our patrons benefit greatly from these features, it is a cost we need to absorb.

With many newer eBooks being created for, integrated with, and loaned through tablets, iPads, and smart phones, we literally have our libraries in our pockets at all times. Catalog search widgets are embedded into our websites and available through apps to satisfy our quick and constant searching impulses. And because students often gravitate toward the Google lookalike search box, an embedded search widget is a handy trick to get them to jump in and search your local catalog first.

In addition, the newest upgrades to most library systems allow patrons to renew items, pay fines, and place holds without staff intervention and with complete privacy. And with library apps on mobile devices, it is possible to do all of these things while waiting in line to order a frappuccino.

Catalogs remain a major player in libraries today and they will still be in the libraries of tomorrow. It is still necessary and important to demonstrate to students how library catalogs and searches are useful for academic and personal purposes. Make the catalog familiar and ubiquitous, and incorporate it into every possible patron access point—embed and add the catalog to your website, research pathfinders, or guides. Take screen shots and create posters to display in your library or to use in tutorials. Make bookmarks with your screen image or use the screen image as your "brand" on overdue and fine notices. Do all that you can to dispel the excuses "I didn't know about the catalog" and "I wasn't taught about the library catalog."

Although you want to use the catalog's search widget to invite and draw students into your catalog, constantly provide instruction on searching your catalog in the advanced mode. Catalogs are a great segue into Boolean operators, truncation, and search punctuation that can be transferred to advanced database searching at a later time. Expect and teach students to use the advanced search methods and don't assume that students have the savvy skills needed to find topics and items that they need and that you take for granted.

Even if you are simply demonstrating and teaching about how to build advanced search strategies, turn the session into an interactive activity. Build a search strategy, run the search, look at the list of results, and go back to the strategy. Ask students to recommend changes, additions, or other ways to get even better or different results. Praise good answers and toss candy to the participants. Help develop the not-so-good answers by asking leading questions and when the student finally arrives at a good strategy, reward him or her as if it was all his or her idea to begin with.

When that topic is exhausted, ask for another student's topic and begin the exercise again. Keep the students engaged by responding to their efforts with energy or small rewards.

At the end of the year, offer the graduating class an opportunity to explore a university's library website and resources. Hold lunchtime college seminars where you demonstrate how they can find books, periodicals, reserve materials, and popular reading items. Create a digital college visit and encourage students to locate an academic librarian's e-mail address, an FAQ page for the library, and the library's operating hours during regular semesters. Contact colleagues from academic institutions and schedule field trips (or electronic field trips with Skype or Facetime) for senior class groups to a local university or college. A welcoming word from a university librarian might lessen worries students have about going off to a larger institution. They might even think fondly of you as they trudge to the library next year.

MEDIA TOOLS, PROGRAMS, AND PLATFORMS

School librarians, often called library-media specialists, have been exploring, using, and teaching about media since the beginning of school library time.

Teachers and students have a well-worn path to the library to learn and use media tools. It's likely that teachers' and students' first introduction to Power-Point, video creation, and digital cameras occurred in the library. And it's likely that the first Animoto videos that popped up in your school had roots in the library.

We have moved past recommending and providing single media programs to our patrons. Today's cast of media players is growing hour-by-hour and category-by-category. We have media tools for presentations, online tutorials, digital scrapbooking and storytelling, images, poster creation, and digital displays. There are media programs to aid with collaboration and social learning. We have social media aggregators that keep all of our social tools in a single and organized space, and some that will create newspapers from the posts we write and read. Students can practice writing, reading, and spelling skills in the comic and graphic novel generators.

Today's learning sometimes feels more like entertainment. The media tools discussed here and in Chapter 7 make research and the assimilation of information from research more interesting and enjoyable for both teachers and students. Help your teachers and school community revolutionize classroom assignments and projects by discovering, demonstrating, and encouraging students to use newer methods that better express their ideas and research results.

Slide Shows and Presentations

When do we decide it's time to change things up and try something new? PowerPoint has been the standard presentation tool for over 20 years. So many media programs are now available to us that perhaps it's time to turn our assignments and presentations in another direction. You can create a fresh new style of presentation with screen recorders, podcasts, playlists, videos, and a combination of media. Most media programs are web tools that live in the cloud and that don't require downloading a big file. They also allow access anywhere at any time. You can use and provide access to your presentation or tutorial when you save it to the cloud, e-mail it to yourself or others, embed it on your website or another website, or upload it to a sharing site.

Screen Recorders

Screen Recorders are useful for posting online presentations as tutorials, demos, or review. There is no need to toss out the well-loved PowerPoint slides in our portfolios and on our hard drives; instead, allow the PowerPoint slides on which we rely to be morphed into a fresher format for independent learning. It's a fairly simple process, with many choices of available screen recording programs that anyone can quickly learn to use. Choose from programs like Knovio (http://www.knovio.com/), SlideRocket (http://www.sliderocket.com/), or

Brainshark (http://www.brainshark.com/) to narrate uploaded slides and to change them into a video recording. These tools record the computer screen as we move through the presentation. And through the webcam on our computer, we become the narrator with our video image appearing unobtrusively in a corner of the screen. These newest screen recorders go a step beyond the tools of yesterday as they provide a face to the presentation and become a more personal aid to users.

For those who are new to audio or video recording, it takes some preparation to ensure that your recordings, which may be played hundreds of times, are as professional as possible. Prepare and work from a script, and do a couple of practice runs so that you don't stumble for words or get lost in your presentation.

For those who just can't or don't want to give up PowerPoint but who want to migrate to a handheld device, creating PowerPoint presentations on an iPad or tablet is easy with the Quickoffice Pro HD app. It is an office-editing suite for the iPad, and you can create and edit Microsoft Office documents, spreadsheets, and presentation formats.

In addition, if you create your PowerPoint slide show on a computer, there are many choices of apps—which are inexpensive or free—that allow you to view or present slide shows on your iPad or tablet. Mobile devices should make us mobile. Lighten the load and leave the heavy laptop at home. If purchasing apps isn't an option, consider using the PowerPoint-like presentation tool in Google Docs, which can be created in Google Drive; upload an existing PowerPoint presentation and convert it to Google's productivity tool.

Screencast-o-matic is another screen recorder with an intuitive interface and a generous free, basic membership. Much like Knovio and other programs mentioned earlier in this chapter, Screencast-o-matic records your computer screen while you narrate with a microphone and/or use your webcam for video. Depending on the acoustic quality of the space where you do your recording, you can use your computer or laptop's mic or a higher quality USB drive plug-in microphone for any of these screen recording programs. Again, existing PowerPoint slides can be uploaded and used, and the narration will bring them to life. Screen recording videos are useful for demonstrating database searches as well as introducing your library catalog or a specific media tool to students who are getting ready to tackle a presentation or assignment. Post your complete recording on the web, or share it through social media or your research pathfinders or guides. Again, it's best to have a script in hand and prepare before going live. Although the free Screencast-o-matic program, as well as the others, offers enough features for most of us and gives users a chance to try out the program, the next subscription level's low annual fee provides many more features that might be important to you. For example, additional features such as unlimited recording time, advanced recorder controls, and the ability to publish in many more file formats, to publish to Google Docs, to edit recordings, and to use a script creator are available if needed or desired. While the free subscriptions might be all that students need, you are likely to want more options.

Prezi

If zooming, panning, and adding YouTube videos, audio, images, PDFs, and text is something that sounds like the type of dynamic presentation you'd like to create, then Prezi might be your tool. Again, you can take your current PowerPoint presentations and use those trusty old slides in Prezi. Your presentation will glide smoothly from information and media selections with the option to add special effects. All the same media that you added to PowerPoint and Keynote can be added to Prezi, but the overall look is new and improved.

PowerPoint masters will learn to use Prezi quickly. I used Prezi as my presentation format to create and show a class of students a demo of Prezi, and most of the students in that class adopted Prezi for their class presentation. And to demonstrate the ease with which Prezi can be learned, the students created and completed their assignment in just a few days. Although the basic Prezi program is free and students can create their own accounts, they offer an upgraded additional free account for educators that allows student access with fuller and additional features. Prezi use and access isn't limited to a laptop or other computer. The Prezi Viewing app for the iPad is even better than Prezi on a computer because while you are presenting, you can scale your details on the screen by stretching and zooming in and out with the pinch technique, or you can pull and push your information around the screen in a very natural way. The newer upgrade to the Prezi app allows you to edit. If an error is discovered in your presentation minutes before your show, you can use the app to quickly make the fix right on your iPad.

Students and teachers in my school are excited about Prezi and its new twist on presentations that seem fresher and more natural. The newest features—including 3D backgrounds and fade-in animations—provide even more reasons to give Prezi a try. One warning for new Prezi presenters: there's a lot of motion within a Prezi presentation, and you'll make your viewers seasick if you aren't careful with your design. But rest assured that Prezi offers some very well-designed and easy-to-follow tutorials for both new and experienced users.

Video Content

Videos are no longer a format for passive classroom viewing. Students and teachers are creating and using videos to teach, complete research projects, present ideas, and showcase events, individuals, or services.

When I need a tutorial for learning how to do something—anything—for example, training a dog, kayaking, adding a calendar to an iPad, explaining what Twitter is, or creating citations in MLA format, I turn to YouTube. I don't think that I've been disappointed by not finding a topic that I needed on YouTube, and there are some very professionally created videos among all of the amateur flicks that include videos created in university departments and libraries.

Video posting sites, some intended for educators and educational purposes, as well as others like YouTube that exist to satisfy any interest, are popping up all over the web. Some of the most popular include Ted Talks, iTunes U, Teacher Tube, and PBS videos. In addition, streaming video databases such as Discovery Education, Learn 360, and Films on Demand provide some of the most trusted and recognized educational videos available, and they are tools that educators are integrating into many classrooms and curricula. Video database subscriptions can be pricey, but they might be worth the cost when you consider that all the content has been reviewed and selected for a learning environment. The search features in these video databases are designed for teachers and students, and the option to use clips instead of the entire video is invaluable for opportunities to reinforce, expand, and enhance instruction or to introduce a concept. In addition, if your teachers have a one-stop-shopping site that they know they can depend on to find what they need when they need it, the demand and value will outweigh the expense.

Using videos in an educational setting begs for classroom discussion and dialogue. Vialogues is a program that provides tools to promote that interaction. Social media tools pair seamlessly with the program to encourage participants and groups to watch, discuss, and comment on a video. Recordings of the online sessions allow for discussions and comments to be saved, embedded, linked on websites, and archived for later review. Vialogues has received much attention and applause. It has been named one of the American Association of School Librarians (AASL)'s Best 2012 Websites for Teaching and Learning. Although the same video presentation and discussion can take place in a traditional classroom in front of a single screen with students and teachers face to face, the technology and social media component of Vialogues offers that novel entertainment quality that students enjoy.

In addition to viewing, discussing, and learning from educational videos, the creation of videos has become popular with students. Clubs, classes, individuals, and teachers are telling their stories through photo video tools such as Animoto (http://www.animoto.com), Stupeflix (http://studio.stupeflix.com), and Flixtime (http://flixtime.com). These top three photo video creation sites offer free versions that allow users to add photos, music, and text to create a video. Although the free accounts usually limit length and have fewer features than the fee accounts, all produce stunning effects with their well-developed, simple, and easily navigated steps. Animoto has been around since 2005 and has gotten better every year. In addition to free 30-second videos anyone can create, Animoto offers free educator accounts with unlimited video length and number of videos that can be produced. The first time I used Animoto was for an open house library presentation at my school in 2006. Since 2006, it has been incorporated it into school-wide events to showcase student trips, student assignments and projects, and all-school assemblies and pep rallies. In addition, I've seen teachers and students using Animoto to create dazzling wedding, birthday, and anniversary video presentations for families and friends.

It took a while for me to consider Animoto as a program for class presentations and projects, but it is now a popular option for students and teachers. Animoto videos can be paused as needed for more explanation or emphasis, or the videos can be played at the beginning or end of a Prezi or PowerPoint presentation for emphasis. A free app for iPad and iPhone is available, and the videos are easily embedded into a website or uploaded to a video site for easy viewing. I've created an Animoto video as a welcome on my website's homepage.

Animoto, Flixtime, and other video slide show creators are so easy to use that I've used them successfully with seven-year-olds in a summer camp setting. In addition to images, titles, and a choice of special effects, students can add their own words and text to provide descriptions, information, and even a bibliography. Videos and music are easily uploaded from Animoto's library or from personal video and music libraries, and students can choose no theme or special themes and templates. And the videos can be remixed until the results match the student's expectation.

Images, Posters, and Digital Displays

Despite all of the digital gadgets and tools we play with and have available in our libraries, sometimes it's a simple paper image, poster, or display that gets the most attention. I have a 22-inch digital monitor in our library with colorful and dynamic daily updates, daily school schedules, announcements, riddles, comics, trivia, grammar tips, photos, and more. I also created a large, laminated, paper 30-inch by 46-inch poster of a chart of social media tools comparisons and contrasts, and have it hanging it on a wall in the library. Guess what cost more, takes daily effort and time, and got a lot less attention? Yes, it's the library display. It could be that it's the location of the display, or maybe it's not large enough (since most of the small-screen TVs we watch at home are more than 37 inches), maybe I'm not hitting the right combination of information, or maybe it's just this particular poster and topic that gained students' attention this one time. Despite the favoritism, I'm not about to give up my digital display, although I might look for a more visible location. However, I will give more credit to simpler and less expensive methods of communication. I'm definitely going back to the Block Poster website (http://www.blockposter.com) where I created that social media poster for just the few pennies that it cost to print out the number of pages that I cropped, cut, and taped together to form the large single poster. In addition,

Block Poster was a favorite tool at the summer technology camp where elementary school students proudly printed and took home a self-portrait to hang on their bedroom walls. Students will think of a million uses for Block Posters, and teachers can create color posters for their classrooms at very little cost.

Word Clouds

It's likely that you've used Wordle (http://www.wordle.net), the online word cloud generator, or that you have come across it in the past few years. Students quickly become addicted to typing or pasting in words and phrases, slogans, or love letters and then trying out different fonts, colors schemes, and directions to make stunning posters of their word collections. Share the following suggestions for using word clouds in a classroom setting with teachers and students:

- Building vocabulary
- Creating spelling tests
- Motivating reluctant writers
- Discovering themes, patterns, and topics
- Studying works of poetry or literature
- Writing poetry or prose
- Studying current or historical events
- Learning and reading famous speeches
- Storytelling
- Creating Icebreakers and introductions
- Studying Music lyrics
- Creating biographies or autobiographies
- Team building
- Reinforcing foreign language instruction
- Creating Classroom signage
- Reinforcing self-esteem

Wordle is the standard for word clouds, but now there is a new kid on the block. Tagxedo (http://www.tagxedo.com) kicks the world of word clouds up a notch. Tagxedo produces visually appealing clouds much like Wordle but also allows those word clouds to be put into a wide variety of shapes and designs. For example, students can use an image of a celebrity or historical figure to create a portrait composed of adjectives or characteristics of the individual. Reluctant writers will suddenly be eager to think of and to key in words to design a new form, and both Wordle and Tagxedo work well as an introductory or ending slide or the background screen during a presentation.

Digital Storytelling Resources

Everyone loves stories. Look what historical fiction has done for awareness of history and historical events, people, and cultures. Who doesn't love *The*

Paris Wife by Paula McLain, *Caleb's Crossing* by Geraldine Brooks, or the Boleyn Sisters series by Philippa Gregory? Historical fiction's purpose seems simple—it adds a colorful story to an event, person's life, or point of view to make it entertaining and more appealing to average readers and learners. You don't have to be a history buff to enjoy learning about the English Reformation, Native American history, or famous authors and the eras in which they lived through historical fiction. Everything taught in any class in any school has a story, or the potential for a story. Every student in every classroom in every school around the world has endless stories waiting to be shared, told, and explored.

Digital storytelling takes traditional storytelling components such as computer generated images and photos, audio recordings and narrations, music tracks, sound effects, text, and video, and turns them into electronic presentations and histories to be shared through social media, presentations, and the web. If a photo can paint a thousand words, than media tools that create digital storytelling should be able to create libraries of stories.

From the StoryCorps (http://storycorps.org) program that has brought much awareness to the radio listening community about the importance of individual stories and voices, to the Educational Uses of Digital Storytelling website, which has amassed just about any digital storytelling resource that an educator might need, a movement for digital storytelling is clearly underway in schools and communities. It is no coincidence that there is an abundance of new media programs that provide the tools, platforms, and ideas to support that interest. Every story, whether based on the same theme or not, is individual and personal to the storyteller, and the shared stories will live on beyond the project.

StoryCorps' National Day of Listening (http://nationaldayoflistening.org) began in 2008 and occurs annually on the day after Thanksgiving. StoryCorps' intent—to have individuals record an interview with a loved one or someone who has made a difference in their life—is an activity and project that can easily be incorporated into a classroom or school library setting. StoryCorps' free "Do-It-Yourself Instruction Guide" provides interviewing techniques and guidelines, advice for choosing recording equipment, and a list of favorite StoryCorps questions to ask. The resources and support from StoryCorps and the National Day of Listening website makes the project a sure-to-succeed adventure for your school. In addition to having current students participate, consider asking current and past teachers, administrators, and alums to provide stories and interviews of personal experiences, exploits, and time at your school. The results will be an invaluable collection of oral history that can be used to teach students and to provide stories about your school. Your advancement department and public relations director might want to be involved in the activities that provide unique, personal stories and opportunities to promote your school. Or expand beyond your school

The Educational Uses of Digital Storytelling website by B. Robin (2012). http://digitalstorytelling.coe.uh.edu.

walls to include the local community; ideas from the National Day of Listening website include sponsoring a program to teach others how to create oral history or providing interview and recording opportunities for them in your school. Groups that might be invited include Rotary clubs, veterans' associations, Boy and Girl Scout troops, homeless shelters, retirement homes, hospices, tutoring or mentoring programs, and arts organizations. At the very least, your library program can coordinate the collaborations among the individuals or departments who might want to take charge of an oral history and digital storytelling project in your school.

The Educational Uses of Digital Storytelling website (http://digitalstory telling.coe.uh.edu), developed by the University of Houston, began in 2004, and it has become a dynamic resource that constantly adds new free content for educators who want to incorporate storytelling into their classroom or school. Their goal from the website indicates that desire clearly:

The Educational Uses of Digital Storytelling website is to serve as a resource for teachers and students who are interested in how multimedia can be integrated into a variety of educational activities . . . Many of the digital stories contained on this site include still images, audio files and video clips that were found using commonly available Internet search engines, websites such as YouTube and Google Video, as well as from commercial VHS tapes and DVDs. One of the main purposes of these digital media projects is to model for educators how they can utilize the power of accessible multimedia to engage students in today's K-12 and higher education classrooms.

—Bernard Robin

Some of the many digital storytelling links and tools that the Educational Uses of Digital Storytelling website provide are basic explanations, overviews, and administrative elements involved in digital storytelling. For example, the website's content and links include suggestions for software and media tools, the elements of digital storytelling, educational uses, goals and objectives, how to get started, creating storyboards and photo collages, rubrics, and standards alignment information.

In addition, storytelling tutorials and media examples that cover any topic or field that you can imagine are offered to users for the simple price of a citation that they provide for users right on the site. For example, over 30 examples of digital storytelling within the topic of pop culture are available. Examples include "The Cost of Fast Food," "My Grandfather," "The Beauty Hidden in Tragedy," "Shopping," and "The World of My Daughter." These and other sample stories can be viewed on a variety of devices that include iPads and Apple or Window computers. If desired, users can download the video. The University of Houston's Educational Uses of Digital Storytelling website offers educators and students use of its resources in order to create opportunities to find stories to tell and report.

Another important resource for digital storytelling tools includes the free eBook *Best Digital Storytelling Examples and Resources* by Richard Byrne, author of the blog Free Technology for Teachers (http://www.freetech4 teachers.com/). Byrne has posted the digital storytelling publication on his blog, and he has been providing it as a free PDF download to educators since January 2012. It's a 76-page publication that's full of step-by-step procedures and digital storytelling successes described by real-life classroom teachers who developed ideas and implemented them for their students. The digital storytelling resources and examples in the book include rubrics, step-by-step procedures, methods, and some broader overviews that describe the purpose and expected outcomes of assignments and lessons. Since Richard's emphasis in his writing and blog is about free resources, many of the recommended tools are free programs or programs that are likely to be available and used in any school or library. Examples of the digital storytelling projects that are included in the eBook are The Grandparents Project, Forever Grateful: A Veteran Interview Project, The Haiku Project, and Sell the Government Back to the American People: A Media Literacy Study of Marketing, Branding, and Advertising.

Again, Byrne's book is offered to educators at no cost, and you can download the PDF to you computer at http://www.freetech4teachers.com/2012/01/free -download-ten-digital-storytelling.html.

If digital storytelling isn't happening yet in your school, begin the trend through the library. Three easy ways to begin digital storytelling are:

1. Collaborate with a teacher(s) to help them launch a project in their classroom.
2. Offer students and teachers an opportunity to create StoryCorps-type interviews in your library and to participate in the National Day of Listening.
3. Promote storytelling media programs in your library. Do a display with a description of digital storytelling, ideas of how to use digital storytelling for a class project or assignment, and some suggestions of media programs that are quick and easy to learn and use for digital storytelling.

Students can create and tell stories in ways other than traditional interviews and audio or video recordings. The following media programs offer tools that can be incorporated into a lesson at a moment's notice, with or without much instruction for users. These engaging programs might be just what reluctant writers and readers need to become interested in the written word. Comic Master (http://www.comicmaster.org.uk) and My Story Maker (http://www .clpgh.org/kids/storymaker/embed.cfm) are two storytelling media programs that were named *School Library Journal*'s (SLJ) Best Websites for Teaching and Learning in 2012.

Comic Master has a bold superhero look and feel with lots of special effect exclamations like "Boom," "Koom," and "Aiiieee" that students will love to add to their stories. The easy-to-use program prompts students to add frames, characters, backgrounds, and dialogue to create multipage graphic novels. Completed stories can be printed, and users who create accounts can save their work to visit or edit at another time. A quick screen shot will create an image of the graphic pages to be added or uploaded to other programs, works, and websites. Accounts are easily created with just an e-mail address and the creation of a password.

The digital storytelling program, My Story Maker, is directed toward a younger audience, with soft and friendly animal characters. When creating a story, the writer controls the character's actions, feelings and emotions, and settings. Animation gives this tool an interactive and visual edge, and users are prompted to add pages, action, and words. The story can be previewed at any point and can be embedded into a website. This storytelling website has many opportunities for young writers to tell their own stories, display their own feelings and emotions, and learn about elements of stories and literature.

A third digital storytelling website recommended as one of SLJ's 2012 Best Websites is Inanimate Alice (http://www.inanimatealice.com). The story of Alice is described as a transmedia project that uses all types of media such as text, images, puzzles, music, and video to pull readers into the story and

Inanimate Alice (www.inanimatealice.com)

engage them. As the Inanimate Alice website states, "Students are encouraged to co-create developing episodes of their own, either filling in the gaps or developing new strands."

The Alice website includes educational resources directed at both parents and teachers with activities, curriculum connections, and ways to share the interactive book with others. This unique digital novel will entice even the most reluctant readers to become immersed in Alice's story, and the continuing episodes keep readers involved and engaged. This book may be best utilized in a classroom setting, but I'm guessing that we'll be seeing Alice book clubs popping up in libraries very soon.

Digital storytelling can take many forms, and it is not essential to include recording equipment, video cameras, or scripts to create autobiographical or biographical stories. Digital scrapbooking, or just paper and photo scrapbooking for that matter, is a simple and traditional method of telling a story. For example, the vacation scrapbook you created for your senior year in high school is a storytelling method that incorporates media. It tells the story of your life as a young adult through photos and text. However, encourage students to bump their scrapbooking up a step or two by using fun digital resources and various types of media to bring it to life and make it entertaining. With these free programs, students and schools can eliminate the cost of paper, glue, and markers. For example, Biteslide (http://www.biteslide.com/) (formerly Beeclip.edu) provides a format for students to create diaries, journals, mood boards, scrapbooks, collages, and portfolios, to name a handful of options from their website. Teachers are offered a free subscription for up to 30 students, and Biteslide's features include a management system for teachers to keep track of students' projects. A no-registration trial is offered so that users can take the site for a spin before registering. Biteslide also provides a handy and useful Nibbler, a downloadable tool or bookmarklet that clips images from the web and stores them in the user's scrapbook for easy access and use.

Jux (https://jux.com) is an irresistible and beautiful digital scrapbooking site that will inspire students. It is developed to be a full website creator, but it appears so much less complicated and technical than any I've seen. At first look, Jux seems to be a site for the combination of scrapbooking and social posting, but it feels more like an art gallery. There are no sidebars, advertising, or buttons to distract users (and especially students). Jux users, with little effort, add images, photos, and words to Jux. Additional features include the ability to create captions and link the images to a webpage. Jux truly is gorgeous, and you will want to figure out ways to use Jux and reasons to look at Jux, and you will certainly encourage others to take a look. Tell your most creative teachers and students about Jux.

Storytelling takes so many different forms, and if these ready-to-go resources don't fit your needs, age group, or community, peruse them at least for inspiration. Take a close look at the features and tools that they provide, and figure out how you can adapt or create similar results to inspire your school players to create any type of digital storytelling. For years, students and teachers have successfully pulled together media projects and storytelling with just a video camera, audio recorder, interview questions, and script. No matter how stories get told—whatever the method or technology used—students will benefit from the process and exposure to storytelling.

COLLABORATION AND SOCIAL LEARNING SPACES

Even the youngest students recognize Twitter, Facebook, Pinterest, and LinkedIn. They see older siblings and parents using them, and they too want to join the fun. Despite the literature that supports and recommends social media as learning tools for the classroom, many schools (high schools too) still block these sites from students—and sometimes even faculty and staff. Admittedly, those sites can be a distraction for students, and it might be difficult to manage security and privacy issues that arise with underage learners. Luckily, for many years now, innovators have been coming to the aid of teachers who want to encourage and cultivate online learning groups, collaborations, and discussion among their students in a secure setting designed specifically for schools and classrooms.

Although I still strongly suggest that social media tools must be used with students in order to teach them how to navigate social networks safely and appropriately, there are many advantages to using the same types of activities in classrooms through social learning spaces such as Blackboard (http://www .blackboard.com/), Edmodo (www.edmodo.com/), Moodle (http://moodle.org/), and Collaborize Classroom (http://www.collaborizeclassroom.com/). These secure spaces provide features similar to the most popular social networking sites. Some secure management systems are pricey, but Edmodo, Moodle, and Collaborize Classroom are free for users.

School Library Journal's (SLJ) 2012 Best Websites for Teaching and Learning recognizes Collaborize Classroom as a tool that brings students and teachers together in an online learning environment. Students are provided online interaction through activities, assignments, and discussion, along with options to vote or to be included in a poll. One of the best features of the Collaborize Classroom is the large library of resources that offer ready-to-go classroom activities within all fields of study for teachers to browse, use, and contribute. For example, if English students in your school study Golding's *Lord of the Flies,* they can participate in an already-created video lecture discussion that has been shared by a member teacher from the Collaborize Classroom community. This particular activity includes the Golding lecture video, a rubric, and discussion points about the novel and video lecture.

The beauty of this site is that the collaboration extends beyond a single classroom, school or district. Teachers collaborate with other teachers by providing lesson plans and activities to enrich students' learning and to engage their learners through media and online conversations.

Mighty Bell (http://mightybell.com/) by Ning co-founder Gina Bianchini was released in April 2012. This site is a collaborative space for individuals and groups to share and discuss common topics, and to create step-by-step guides to the resolution of a problem or issue. Text, photos, and documents can be added to pages, and the pages can be saved as a webpage with a URL to share. Although not designed with the educational world in mind, the features that allow and promote group and individual pages can be utilized for secure classroom settings. Pages can be private, by invitation only, or open to the entire web community. And happily, there is a mobile app in the works.

SOCIAL MEDIA CURATORS AND AGGREGATORS

Using social media information sources like Twitter, Facebook, Pinterest, and blogs are invaluable and enlightening, but they can also be a time stealer. It takes time to read, interpret, and imagine what to do with the information that we discover through the social web. The experts that we rely on to provide us with the newest tools, trends, and philosophies are producing, posting, and announcing information constantly in real time. Miss a week while on vacation, and you might miss the single best piece of information that was pushed to you in the past couple of months. We all need to unplug and take a vacation to the beach or just away from work, and social aggregators help us by collecting and storing our selected sources for us to access at a later time. Social aggregators can be Really Simple Syndication (RSS) readers that list the information and sources to which you subscribe, or they can create graphic publications from the posts within each subscription site that you follow. Most blog and social networking aggregators are free tools with some fairly sophisticated features available to users. For example, the Google Reader (http://www.google.com/reader) that comes with a Google Gmail or Drive account is the one-stop-shopping type of aggregator that lists all the blogs to which you subscribe. Simply subscribe from a specific blog's website by selecting the RSS feed option. Select your aggregator from the list that appears, and the blog will then appear in your aggregated list of blogs. Google Reader also provides a service beyond being your reading site for your blogs—you can feed Google Reader terms or words that describe your personal or professional interests, and items that match your terms will be curated and pushed to your Google Reader site. Other free RSS readers and aggregators that perform similar services are Feedburner (http://feedburner.google.com/), Feedreader (http://www.feedreader.com/), Bloglines (http://www.bloglines.com/), SharpReader (http://www.sharpreader.net/), and NewsGator (http://www.newsgator.com/).

Allow aggregators to become your good friends by streamlining the process of reading and keeping up with all of your social networks. Beyond blog readers, there are aggregators to manage your other social networks such as Twitter and Facebook. These aggregator sites provide many more features and personal management options that include scheduling both outgoing and incoming posts, filtering, and designing the look and feel of the interface. Become more efficient by using one of the following tools to read multiple social network feeds from a single location.

Summify (http://summify.com/), recently acquired by Twitter, uses artificial intelligence to choose, pull, and summarize the most relevant information from your Twitter, Facebook, and Google Reader networks, and to deliver it to you through mobile devices, e-mail, or on the web. Instead of rolling through all posts to determine what you want to stop to read, Summify makes those choices for you.

TweetDeck (http://www.tweetdeck.com/) is an app that aggregates feeds from multiple networks and sites. The mobile app manages Twitter and Facebook networks, and the Web version of TweetDeck provides management of additional networks such as Foursquare and LinkedIn.

HootSuite (www.hootsuite.com/) provides management of up to five social networking sites, message scheduling, quick reports, and two RSS feeds with the free account. The upgraded Pro account provides many more features, and a 30-day free trial is available.

GRAPHIC CONTENT AGGREGATORS

There are many graphic content aggregators that provide similar information-gathering services as discussed in the preceding section but that go a step further by gathering and generating the posts and information into a graphic product or publication. You can publish your blog, Twitter, and Facebook posts all in the same place at the same time, and share your graphic publication across social platforms. For example, Paper.li (http://paper.li/) is a content curation service that publishes an online newspaper based on an individual's choices, interests, and posts from social networking sites. Publications can be scheduled on a regular cycle that is determined by the user and easily set up under settings or on an as needed basis. Specific news or topical items can be selected or deselected and prioritized, or users can allow the featured items for the publication to be automatically selected for them. Use Paper.li to create a slick library newsletter publication using your library Twitter, Facebook, and blog posts. The newsletter will include your library's announcements, recommendations, and information that you have recently Tweeted or shared with your community and followers, and the publication will look like it took hours, days, or weeks to produce. Let this new and sophisticated newsletter replace the print or word-processed library newsletter of yesterday, and be prepared for questions about how you created, or had time to create, such a polished publication.

Along with social networking feed aggregators, Graphic content aggregator apps for your tablet, iPad, or other mobile device are storming the mobile device scene. Flipboard (http://flipboard.com/) is an iPad and iPhone app that consistently shows up on "best recommended" lists for apps. It provides a glossy magazine-style publication full of images, photos, and videos that are pulled from your Tweets, Facebook account, Instagram, YouTube, Flickr, and other newsfeed and timelines accounts. You can easily add content and topics from Flipboard's suggestions and content lists. To become a Flipboard fan, simply flip through a couple of pages of your account, and you will be hooked. Flipboard is as attractive as they come, and it is always fun and a little shocking to open up your account and see a photo of you, a family member, friends, or colleagues pop up within the glossy format.

Use and recommend these various styles and types of aggregators to teachers and students so that social media platforms become part of organizing busy digital lives. Students will be drawn to the visual displays created by these aggregators, and they will likely want to create curated sites and graphic publications of what they are studying and learning for class projects. Students will be so engaged with creating a visually appealing project that the content of the class—and the technological knowledge and skills that they develop and learn—will happen happily and easily.

Perhaps you are already a social networking believer and participant, but you're not sure how to best share your own social networking posts in order to grow your followers and readership. The resources that we use for patron access and resources are perfect sites that can double as locations where our social networking feeds appear. Library websites, research pathfinders and guides, and wikis are natural places to embed your library's Twitter, LinkedIn, or Facebook feeds. In addition, add RSS feeds from blogs with related topics to the sites that students visit or use for research purposes. For example, while creating a research tool, pathfinder, or guide for an alternative energy research assignment, find and add an RSS news feed from a database or blog. And if students are studying careers in the science field, embed news feed to a science careers blog or to the newest issue of a science magazine with highlighted careers. Finally, if students are studying British literature, add an RSS feed to a blog about British authors and themes about classic literature.

Finding educational websites and resources has been part of school librarians' informal or formal job description since the World Wide Web became part of our daily lives. The web isn't getting any smaller, and it can be difficult to find time to peruse and select websites for students and teachers. However, free graphic curation tools like Scoop.it (http://www.scoop.it/), Storify (http://storify.com/), Redux (http://redux.com/), BagTheWeb (http://bagtheweb.com/), and Bundlr (http://bundlr.com/) are created to make that job easier. They are aids to pull together groups of related websites or social media feeds to share with others or to keep in ready reference. These curation tools provide quick links for posting to social media sites, and most programs provide a downloadable bookmarklet that appears in a browser's toolbar. Click on the bookmarklet when selecting a website or contents, and—instantly and seamlessly—the site finds its way to the group that has been indicated.

REAL-TIME COLLABORATION TOOLS SHRINK A LARGE SPACE

Let's move out of the classroom for a moment and into a professional setting with colleagues. Take a close look at the collaboration tools discussed in this section if you or someone else in your school is planning a presentation or lecture. We've all experienced how interaction and discussion during presentations in a large and overcrowded room can sometimes be difficult, even for the most experienced presenter. But Today's Meet (http://todaysmeet.com/) and Backchan.nl (http://backchan.nl/) are two platforms that involve live audiences with voting, feedback, answering questions, and providing comments within a group setting. These collaboration tools are likely to make that large hall feel more intimate and focused.

Today's Meet requires little preparation and takes only four steps to get every person involved in the live stream: enter a room name, add your name or alias, select how long you want the session to be saved, and click on Create a Room. The messaging screen is so simple that even novices will find it easy to use. Messages are limited to a familiar 140 characters. Demonstrate these presentation tools to teachers and administrators at your next faculty or school meeting or in-service to test and show how well these tools work in encouraging more participation from the crowd, and then remind your collegues to take one of the tools on the road with them to their next presentation.

Keeping a class of students focused in a smaller space is sometimes difficult as well. To see how eager students are to respond, give a clicker a try next time you provide instruction in the library. The Socrative app (http://www.socrative .com/), which is specifically designed for classrooms settings, is available in both student and teacher versions. The app provides individuals opportunities to engage through educational exercises and games, and it has a platform for polling, voting, and real-time responses. Interaction is provided along with some premade activities that can be used as they are or adapted for individual need. Socrative suggests the following:

> Engage the class, make thinking visible, capture data, save time on grading, and works on any device with a web browser: tablets, smartphones, and Apps. Use Soc- rative for Short Answer Questions: Ask an open-ended question. Students respond and all their answers populate your screen for projection. Then ask students to vote on their favorite and watch the results come in. Space Race: Teams of students answer multiple-choice questions in this fast-paced game. First team to get their rocket across the screen wins! You'll get a graded report. Exit Tickets: Get a quick, paper-free pulse-check at the end of class. All answers are aggregated into a report. Quick Quiz: A teacher paced or student paced activity with multiple choice and/or short answer questions that can be exported to a report that is automatically aggre- gated and graded. Multiple Choice: Ask a MC question, and see student responses on the projection screen as a bar chart.

PIN IT

The most simple concept of all social networking platforms has to be the bulletin board display where users simply pin, or stick, information on a digital space to share with others. Pinterest (http://pinterest.com/) is likely to be the favorite at the moment. Visual theme-based collections curated by individuals or groups are pinned to the board with options for discussion and comments. Students are already using Pinterest for personal interests, and this resource would be a great classroom activity or tool for a digital discussion of a theme or topic. A download- able pin tool, or bookmarklet, allows users to pin any website, image, or part of a website right to their board. With brief, right to the point information that can usu- ally be explored further with a single click, I consider Pinterest to be the visual half-sibling to Twitter's microblogging platform. Create an account for your library and post your resources, research tips and tricks, and favorite library blog posts to demonstrate how digitally savvy the library is.

Another bulletin board service that provides users the ability to post notes col- laboratively and socially is the website Corkboardme (http://corkboard.me).

Managing clubs and committees, planning events, and organizing details are easy and basic with Corkboard.me. Drag and drop files from your desktop, and watch the immediate changes that appear as you, your coworkers, or students add, remove, or change the content. Visual learners will benefit from the corkboard imagery and the colorful notes. Free subscriptions with unlimited notes and real-time updating are provided, but if you want more sophisticated features such as team chat, image and photo ability, encryption, and cloud storage, there is a low monthly price. Take it for a spin with the 30-day free trial and discover how you can use it in your library or for clubs and event planning.

6

There Is an App for That and That and That

What an easy concept—an application that solves a need. Today, tomorrow, and in the immediate future, apps are making our personal and professional lives more efficient and entertaining. Will there be life without apps ever again? There are apps for education, business, productivity, education, entertainment, music, games, social networking, news, sports, travel, news, and lifestyle. There are numerous categories of iPad apps that hold more than 800,000 apps from which we can choose to purchase or install for free. If that seems like a big number, consider that the figure is today's count—tomorrow's count will be much, much higher.

Luckily, there are also hundreds and thousands of blogs, websites, articles, and app reviewers that are making it easier for us to find and determine which ones are the most useful for us to use then recommend to our students and patrons.

Let's look at some apps that have been selected as the best of their category or type. Our natural inclination as school librarians is to focus on educational apps intended for use in classroom or for students, but I urge you to look beyond those educational apps and to also become an expert in many popular (and pop culture) categories and areas. For example, the free iPad app Zillow, a high-resolution real estate app that provides estimated home values, rental prices, and currently listed homes for sale, isn't likely to appear in any best educational app list. However, Zillow can be used when students are studying and working to understand economic issues. The abundance of data, figures, numbers, mortgage calculators, and maps that Zillow provides can easily become a device for a math, economics, or life skills classes. A relevant, meaningful, real-world experience for students might be missed if users don't imagine more for Zillow than house hunting.

Treat apps as any other tool or content that you provide and recommend to your patrons or students. Create and keep an annotated library of recommended apps to give to students, teachers, and colleagues, and display an "App of the Week" or a collection of suggested apps that meet the needs of a specific assignment or project. Tweet your hand-selected or newly released apps to your followers. Add your recommendations and suggestions to a wiki, research pathfinder, or guide then ask your students and patrons to offer their own suggestions.

The alphabetized and annotated list in this chapter, which is not created with only the education or school world in mind—and which I've gleaned from personal experience, teacher recommendations, professional recommendations, websites, Apple's app store, billboards, Starbuck's free giveaways, and any other place I've seen or heard apps advertised or discussed—provides a starting point for discovering how apps can be useful for you and your patrons. In addition, I have installed and tested all of the listed apps and find them worthy of inclusion in this small and selective group. Most of the apps mentioned in this chapter are free or inexpensive, and some apps are currently available only on specific devices or operating systems. But at the speed at which apps are developing beyond their original market for universal use, it's likely that by the time you read this, most of these popular apps will be available for all devices and operating systems.

APP PRICES

Free—indicated
$—Under $10
$$—Over $10

3D Brain by Cold Spring Harbor Laboratory (Free)

Students are able to rotate and zoom into regions and structures of the brain to see how it is affected by mental illness, injury, and disease. There is a lot of praise for the references within this free app, although some reviewers have stated that they would love to see even more detail in the images. But this app is definitely worth a close look for science students and teachers.

3D Cell Simulation and Stain Tool by Invitrogen Corporation (Free)

Students can explore a 3D cell and create their own cell image with this educational app. This free app provides zoom and rotation features so that students can study cell structures. There are over 250 images to experience and explore.

AccuWeather for iPad by AccuWeather, Inc. (Free)

This free interactive app provides weather details and features. Storm warnings and severe weather forecasts are pushed to you, and you can translate everything into multiple languages. The lifestyle forecast page is an interesting and possibly very useful feature that helps you determine what activities might or might not be best for you to participate in for the day, given the weather forecast. This is a useful classroom tool that can be adapted for just about any subject area that involves geography, cultures, or other topics related to climate.

App Shopper by App Shopper, LLC (Free)

This is the very first app that you should download to your iOS device. It will keep you aware of new and updated apps of interest as well as apps that are on sale or being offered for free. Follow App Shopper on Twitter (@appShopper) to make certain you see the newest recommended apps as quickly as they are announced or released.

ARTouch by Kiwilab (Free)

This app is a comprehensive mobile art encyclopedia. Over 3,000 artists and over 24,000 paintings or sculptures from 1000 AD to 1800 AD are searchable, or they can be found through a menu-style index. The advance search feature provides options for searching by art forms or types, or through timelines. The app was created for the iPhone, and although I love the content and format, it is a little buggy on an iPad. Use it on the iPhone or iPod Touch, and wait for an upgrade for the iPad.

Athan: Prayer Timings and Tracking by Islamic Finder (Free)

For personal use or for global studies, this app will provide prayer reminders, directions to a nearby mosque, and location tools to find the qibla direction. Users can log prayers in a personalized prayer book, and some game elements such as badges and scores are also available to users.

Big Picture by Globe Newspaper Company, Inc. ($)

The photo blog from Boston.com uses photographs to present news information from around the world. News updates are posted on Mondays, Wednesdays, and Fridays. The Big Picture app is a great way to begin classroom discussions and to engage students through visual representations of current events.

Bloomberg for iPad by Bloomberg Finance LP (Free)

Gain access to financial markets, business news, and data. Podcasts from Bloomberg radio are available, as are tools to track companies and indexes over time. This is likely to be a useful tool for economics, business, and lifestyles classes.

Complete Class Organizer: Student Version by AnimalBrainz Inc. ($)

This is an intuitive app for students who need or want to organize their academic life. The app's features include note taking, an audio recording tool, and time management and structure for preparing for tests, quizzes, and homework. Other features include drawing, sharing notes with others, and links to Dropbox and Google Docs. Links to websites, teacher e-mails, and class management tools and resources can be added for easy access. Teachers and students in our school love and use this app regularly.

Dictionary.com by Dictionary.com, LLC (Free)

Content in this app comes from Dictionary.com and Thesaurus.com. What's great about this app is that it works without an Internet connection. While reading on their iPads, students—with or without Internet access—can look up words right on the spot without walking across the room to a print dictionary.

Documents to Go by DataViz, Inc. ($-$$)

You can sync local Microsoft Office files and documents from your computer and connect to cloud services such as Google Docs, Dropbox, Box.net, Sugar-Sync, and iDisk. Use this app to view, edit, or create office files on your mobile device.

Driver's Ed* by Brainscape (Free)

Most of your student population will benefit form this app at some point in their high school years. This collection of flashcards and visuals covers the most common rules and regulations form driver's ed tests across the United States. Lots of tips on defensive driving are included.

Dropbox by Dropbox (Free)

One of the most useful and popular cloud storage services. It allows users to sync information, photos, videos, and documents. No more need to e-mail documents to yourself or to carry around a USB jump drive. Access your information anywhere that you have Internet service. 2 GB of storage is provided with the free account.

EBay for iPad by EBay, Inc. (Free)

Think beyond the typical uses of EBay, and consider the useful sociology, economics, and consumer issues and topics hidden in the shopping site. And the app is such a step up from EBay's website that EBay users need to know about it. Is your school looking for fresher fundraising ideas? Consider an EBay rummage sale—little work and big audience.

Edmodo by Edmodo (Free)

The Edmodo website is a classroom management tool, which was developed to keep users connected through mobile iOS devices. Teachers can post assignments, notices, and alerts; lead classroom discussions; and post messages. Students can submit assignments and messages to classmates and teachers.

Educreations Interactive Whiteboard by Educreations, Inc. (Free)

Just about anything you can do on a white board, you can do with this app. Use Educreations to create video tutorials with a touch, tap, and recorded voice. Share the creations or tutorials by posting them to a social networking site. Possible uses for the app include remote tutoring, a flipped classroom setting, or virtual research help.

The Elements: A Visual Exploration by Touch Press ($)

This app is really an eBook that presents the periodic table in an interactive experience. It has been developed specifically for the iPad, and it makes the most of the high-resolution screen and touch technology features. Elements come to life through animation and 3D images. Although somewhat pricey as far as apps go ($6.99), it's a bargain when you consider that it's truly an interactive eBook.

Energy Footprint by Denis Gracanin (Free)

This app is a critical thinking and mathematical problem-solving game that combines players' skills and creativity in a supposed Mid-Atlantic home. Each level of a house has six rooms, and players face challenges to decrease their energy footprint in order to increase their budgets. Science students will love playing the game while developing knowledge and skills.

Epicurious by Conde Nast Digital (Free)

This food app is well developed and practical. I loved Epicurious on my iPhone (it's so easy to have an instant list of ingredients when you are in the grocery store), but viewing the recipes on an iPad in full color and a larger screen is incredible. Browse, search by ingredient, search by keyword, and share recipes and shopping lists through social networks—all in one place. Epicurious is a useful app for students who are learning about food preferences and customs in foreign countries.

Evernote by Evernote (Free)

A popular free app that allows users to take notes, create task lists, record voice reminders, and save photos and websites. This app also syncs your information across all of your devices.

Explore Flickr by Shiny Development (Free)

Flickr fans take note that the Explore Flickr app will use the iPad's high definition to make Flickr images pop out and seem even more vibrant. Images can be downloaded right to your iPhone or iPad photo libraries for easy use.

Facebook by Facebook, Inc. (Free)

What can we say? Facebook isn't going away, and this app provides better resolution for photos. Go get it.

Feeddler RSS Reader for iPad by C.B. Liu (Free)

If you use Google Reader as your RSS reader or aggregator, you'll want this app for your iPad. Simply point the app to your Google Reader, and you'll have your blogs and information on the go.

Find My iPhone by Apple (Free)

This app should be one of the first few apps that you download to a new device. If you misplace a device, another Apple device can be used to locate it by choosing to display a message or play a sound. You can see your device on a visual map, and you can also remotely lock a missing device or erase the data.

There are some entertaining stories floating around the Internet about how Find My iPhone has found devices that were lost or stolen.

Flipboard by Flipboard, Inc. (Free)

This is likely the most visually pleasing and enjoyable social media aggregator available today. Flipboard displays news stories based on what's being shared by you or your friends in Twitter or Facebook, and auto-formats them into a magazine-style platform. You can scan the headlines and first couple of paragraphs then click through to the site to open the full story right in the built-in web browser in the app. You can add websites or people to follow from Flipboard's suggestions. It's always fun and a little surprising to see your own post or photo published on a Flipboard page.

Goodreads by Goodreads (Free)

The Goodreads app gives users mobile access to their Goodreads account, as well as more than a few hundred million books, reviews, and recommendations through other readers' accounts. Walking out of your public library with your latest find under your arm, you can post the title to your book list and share it with your followers.

Google Earth by Google, Inc. (Free)

The Google Earth app is likely to be on the top 10 of any best of the best app list, and it deserves to be there. Viewed from a tablet or iPad, Google Earth makes for sharp visualizations and is so many steps above the computer program. Students can locate borders, cities, and historical landmarks, and tour the world with the 3D imagery and tour guide. The app is useful for global, geography, history, and cultural studies, as well a guide for traveling.

GRE Flash Cards App by TaptoLearn Software (Free for a limited time)

This app is a vocabulary builder with over 1,800 words to help learners ace the GRE or as a high school classroom tool. Quizzes, reminders, and a daily plan will help organize users' learning.

The Guardian Eyewitness by Guardian News and Media Limited (Free)

This news app provides news and sporting events seen through a camera lens. Stunning photographs are the visual representation of global events, and with a single tap, users will be provided with a caption or information regarding a photo. Don't miss the original picture of the day series provided free to users.

iA Writer by Information Architects, Inc. ($)

iA Writer allows a mobile device to be used more easily as a word processor, editor, and document creator. Text (.txt) documents can be formatted easily without a mouse, and completed docs can be synced quickly and easily between a Mac, iPad, and iPhone, and uploaded to iCloud and Dropbox. iA Writer is a useful tool for using iPads in classes where students will want or be required to create written documents.

iBooks by Apple (Free)

A well-designed eBook reader that also works as a newsstand and PDF reader. The reader provides many options for page appearance and also offers a text to speech option. iBooks is an app that your students should have loaded on their iOS devices.

iM+ by SHAPE Services (Free)

Just about any messaging service that you use will be compatible with this app. If you chat or message through Yahoo, Skype, Google, Facebook, Twitter, AIM, or others, you'll find this single platform helpful for bringing it all together in a single place. This app should be useful for teachers when managing online discussion in classroom situations where students are using different services, or as a virtual reference desk to help student with research issues.

IMDb by IMDb (Free)

IMDb is the world's single largest collection of movie, TV, and celebrity information. Use this app as a tool to check out which version of a movie is available on DVD, Blu-ray, or as a digital download. The app also provides reviews, show times, and theater information.

Infinote Pinboard for Tasks and Notes by Jeybee ($)

Visual learners will love this graphic note maker, brainstorming, and time management tool. Colorful notes populate the screen, and with the high resolution available on most tablets, it's impressive.

iTunes U by Apple (Free)

iTunes U looks like entertainment and works like education. Users are provided access to university courses and free educational content that includes assignments and updates from instructors. Choose from over 500,000 free lectures, videos, books, and other resources. Teachers can add iTunes U courses and videos to their curriculum then assign them for homework or use them in class.

Khan Academy by Khan Academy (Free)

It's likely that you are familiar with Khan Academy's large library of educational videos, but the app takes that free content and makes it mobile. Subtitles with a timeline are available for most videos so that viewers can skip ahead to specific clips of interest. The high resolution provides very attractive videos.

Kindle by AMZN Mobile LLC (Free)

The Kindle book reader might do the best job of any book reader by syncing between multiple devices—Kindle Reader, iPad, iPhone, Android phones, PC, Mac, and more. However, one downside to the books borrowed from libraries through the Kindle app is that the book and your borrowing records never truly disappear from Amazon and the Kindle app interface.

Leafsnap by Columbia University, University of Maryland, and Smithsonian Institution (Free)

The science department in our school has been using this app for quite a while, and the students have really benefited from the activities. Leafsnap is a free interactive field guide for leaves, flowers, fruit, bark, and seeds that grow primarily in the Northeast United States. The recognition software is very accurate.

Louvre HD by Musee du Louvre (Free)

Although there have been smart phone apps for the Louvre for a while, the release of the iPad's Louvre HD app kicks it up a couple of notches. Photos of 150 of the Louvre's most popular masterpieces are provided along with over 500 other works of art that can be zoomed into to see tiny details. Images are high resolution, and museum experts provide informative descriptions and explanations for the works. The app also provides a virtual tour of the Louvre itself. Students will feel as though they can visit the Louvre without leaving the classroom, and this app might even entice both students and teachers to put Paris and the Louvre on their bucket lists.

Math Ref by Happy Maau Studios, LLC ($)

The reference app for math topics provides over 1,000 formulas, tips, equations, and concept examples. Features include editable notes, saving equations, and the ability to switch from landscape to portrait mode and back.

Molecules by Sunset Lake Software (Free)

View and manipulate 3D renderings of molecules using the iPad's touch screen. Teachers and students will experience a more interactive study of molecules than ever before.

Monster Anatomy HD by Monster Minds Media SAS ($$)

The intended audience for this series of anatomy apps is healthcare practitioners and professionals—and the highly detailed and accurate images attest to that. But science and anatomy students will also benefit from the high-quality images, information, and features. The series of apps focus on different areas of human body anatomy. The app that I viewed is for the lower leg. This app is pricier than most but well worth it for serious anatomy students.

Movies by Flixter by Flixter (Free)

Find local movie times, theaters, summaries, reviews, and trailers on this easy-to-use app. You can even sync it with your Netflix queue to stream movies.

MythBusters HD by Phunware, Inc. ($)

This Discovery Channel app was created specifically for the iPad. Users can watch MythBusters videos while chatting live through Twitter Chat. This app also features gaming in multilevel formats. Many students love the TV show *Myth Busters*, and they will be excited about using this app in science classes. This is a tool that brings pop culture into the classroom and will make science topics relevant to students' lives and learning.

NASA by NASA Ames Research Center (Free)

On-demand videos, live streaming, and the thousands of images are enough to grab anyone's attention, but add all of the content, launch schedules, and satellite information, and this app becomes a classroom lesson plan. Science teachers and students will benefit greatly.

Nearpod by Panarea (Free)

This classroom app is an easy and dynamic tool for teachers to share content and presentations with students. PDF documents—which might include Power-Point presentations saved as PDFs—are easily uploaded, and students can follow the presentation with their own devices then draw or make notations right on the document. Teachers can manage students' content and devices, and the app's features include assessment, polling, and quiz tools.

NPR by NPR (Free)

The NPR News app is a news source that offers audio podcasts along with print information. It is presented in a magazine format with a focus on news, the arts, and music. Users can curate a playlist, and it's a good source for the discussion of current news topics for the classroom.

OnScreen DNA Model by OnScreen Science, Inc. ($)

Who wants to play with DNA? Science teachers and students do, and they will enjoy the 3D images and animation that this inexpensive app provides. Beautiful and interactive, OnScreen DNA Model will make the science classroom fun and provide an obvious tool for flipping classroom instruction.

PaperDesk Lite for iPad by WebSpinner, LLC ($)

This is an app designed to create digital notebooks, and the intent appears to be to maintain the look and feel of a print notebook. Users can draw, type, and add photos or images to a personally created notebook. Students might prefer this simple and easy-to-use program. However, with the Lite version, users are limited to three pages for each notebook. Pages can be exported to Dropbox, Google Docs, e-mail, Twitter, and AirPrint.

PCalc Lite by TLA Systems Ltd. (Free)

This calculator app adds and edits constants, and there are options for Engineer and Programmer pack. This is an all-around good and basic free calculator.

Penultimate by Evernote ($)

Use Penultimate to take notes with your own handwriting, create sketches, write music, add and edit photos, make lists, or play games such as tic-tac-toe. It's likely that the free paper design options will be all that you and students will ever need, but musicians might want to invest in the music paper options.

A nice feature of Penultimate is that your completed design, document, or work can be quickly and easily printed, e-mailed, and saved to iCloud, Dropbox, Evernote, or other Cloud storage services.

Photoshop Touch by Adobe Systems Inc. ($)

With this app from Adobe, users can use professional editing features and share photos through social media sites like Facebook, Pinterest, and Twitter. You can also sync files to Adobe's Creative Cloud to open in Photoshop on your computer.

Photon Flash Video Player & Private Web Browser for iPad by Appsverse, Inc. ($)

This app is a solution for iPad users who want to utilize LibGuides, Flash games or videos, or websites. Simply use this browser and click on the lightning icon to view flash utilities.

Pinnacle Studio by Corel Inc. ($$)

Pinnacle Studio, formerly Avid Studio, is a full movie-making program that can't be any easier for students to learn and use. The app finds the videos, music, and photos on your iPad and makes selections as simple as tapping and dragging. Special effects and transitions make every video creation look professional and slick. Students will love the simplicity and the results.

Pocket Heart 2 by Pocket Anatomy ($)

This real-time 3D beating heart app gives students a close up view of how the human heart works and sounds. This app can be used without wi-fi or 3G access, and it provides interactive materials such as quizzes, multimedia, and self-paced learning options.

ProPublica by ProPublica (Free)

ProPublica is a nonprofit publication of investigative reporters whose mission is to expose abuses of power by government, business, and other institutions. This is a most useful app for teaching media literacy and for exposing students to the nonprofit side of journalism and news.

Readability by Readability, LLC (Free)

Readability is a web content reader that strips away ads and other distracting material from articles and web information. You can save articles to read later, and you can make notes or comments to share with teachers or students. Another great feature is that you can post information or articles on Twitter or Facebook in one easy step.

Real Animals HD by PROPE (Free-$)

This app's 3D images will bring animals right into your classroom or library. Users will learn about specific animals' habitats, hear the pronunciation of an animal's name, and interact with the animals by making them jump, run, and make sounds. This app is geared toward younger students, and the free version is loaded with ads. It might be worthwhile to invest a few dollars in the upgrade so that you will have clean navigation.

Scrabble by Electronic Arts ($)

Whether you have spare time to fill or you play competitively with friends, Scrabble is one of the original social games and tools. This educational app can be played by the youngest of students. Turn this game app into a classroom activity by suggesting to a history teacher with a unit about the Civil War that she have students play each other with the guidelines that every word played must be related to events, people, or trivia from that era.

ShowMe Interactive Whiteboard by Easel (Free)

Use this iPad app as an interactive white board that integrates audio recordings, images and photos, and drawings. Use ShowMe to create tutorials for your school library and share your presentations on social networks. Students will love the versatility and find reasons to use it for classes.

Show Me on an Apple by Daniel Testerman (Free)

I wish I had an app like this for my everyday life and activities. This tutorial app for all things Apple provides videos and step-by-step instructions for how to set up Apple devices, setup wi-fi, take a screenshot, add keyboard shortcuts, manage iCloud storage, and more.

Skeletal 3D Anatomy by USmau02 ($)

Students and teachers gain access to 3D images of the 206 bones in the human anatomy. Images rotate and zoom with a single swipe of the finger, and reference information is provided along with the images. This is a nice buy for less than a dollar.

Skeptical Science by Shine Technologies (Free)

This free app that focuses on global warming and uses scholarly literature to provide reliable data that will encourage students to think critically and to question what they see and hear. This app was developed for the iPhone and iPod Touch, so the format isn't enhanced by the iPad, but it is still an interesting tool to use in the classroom.

Skitch for iPad by Evernote (Free)

Skitch is a screen-grab and annotation tool. Use arrows, shapes, and text on images, maps, and web pages. Users can also see their work viewed in real time through AirPlay on Apple TV.

Skype for iPad by Skype Communications S.a.r.l (Free)

Call, video call, or message anyone with a Skype account. This app is universal and even though the iPad has Facetime loaded right out of the box, if you've used and become accustomed to Skype, there is no real reason to switch.

Skyview Free by Terminal Eleven LLC (Free)

This powerful and free app packs in any feature that I can imagine is needed for students to study astronomy. It combines 3D effects of the moon, sun, stars, and constellations. Users can point the camera to the sky to identify the sky's stars, visible planets, constellations, and satellites. A very cool and useful feature allows users to change the date and time in order to get a glimpse of future or past astronomic activity and events. Information and facts to support the images are provided, and a gyroscope is available for some devices. This is an ideal app to use with students in tablet orientations to demonstrate the potential of iPad learning or to kick off an astronomy research assignment in the library.

Smithsonian Channel for iPad by Smithsonian Networks (Free)

This app is a mobile gateway to the huge Smithsonian video collection. There are social sharing capabilities with Twitter, Facebook, and e-mail, and a channel finder to check out on-air schedules and availability. However, don't get fooled into thinking that this app provides full episodes of the entire Smithsonian video collection—only a select sampling is available on a rotating basis.

Sock Puppets by Smith Micro Software, Inc. (Free)

Sock Puppets has so much potential to make students laugh, create, and discover their inner writer and performer. This app can be used for storytelling, writing, or foreign language lessons. Groups can work together to have conversations among multiple puppets. Students provide the dialogue and voices, and the puppets lip sync the conversation.

Sound Hound by Sound Hound, Inc. (Free)

This music recognition and lyrics app identifies music playing from a speaker (or even humming), and it provides artist information and lyrics for iPod music. Students who are studying contemporary poetry or music lyrics will love this app.

Star Walk for iPad: Interactive Astronomy Guide by Vito Technology Inc. ($)

Simply point your iPad at the stars, constellations, and satellites in the sky, and the Star Walk app will quickly identify them for you. The graphics and content are very good.

Stop Motion Studio by CATEATER, LLC ($)

Students will love making stop motion animation videos to complete assignments and projects. They'll also love using the app just for fun. The Stop Motion Studio is easy to use—it's possible that the program is harder to stop using than to learn to use. I'm already thinking of things to create for my library.

StoryKit by ICDL Foundation (Free)

Create a story, rewrite one of the four public domain books on the app, or write reviews of a book or movie in a storybook format. Students of all ages will find the features of StoryKit engaging. Drawings, photos and images, text, sound clips, and effects can be uploaded and used to create or enhance a story. Although this app works well on an iPad, it was developed for the iPod Touch and iPhone, so iPad users might be disappointed that the app doesn't take advantage of the larger and higher-resolution tablet screen.

TED Books by TED Conferences (Free)

The TED Books app gives you a platform for purchasing and reading short eBooks produced by Technology, Entertainment and Design (TED) that are inspired by the TED Talks. The books are short and inexpensive, and audio, video, and social media features are embedded into the books. These short books that are full of engaging media might be a great way to introduce a topic to students. Books can be purchased individually, or users can subscribe and receive a new book every two weeks.

TED Talks by TED Conferences (Free)

It's likely that you've already discovered the Technology, Entertainment and Design (TED) Talks, and that you've recommended them to teachers. But don't forget to suggest that the app be added to mobile devices so that students can easily be assigned a talk or two for homework, or as an assignment for a flipped classroom setting. The app allows a playlist to be curated, built, and saved for future viewing.

Teen Age Survival by BD Digital Inc. (Free)

This app should be in all libraries' reference apps collections. Students looking for or asking about information on adolescence, puberty, emotions, and survival tactics for teens should be directed to this free app. In addition, parents, teachers, and anyone who interacts with teens on a regular basis might find this a helpful source.

Things by Cultured Code GmbH & Co. KG ($-$$)

Thing is a task manager above all others (especially free ones.) The intuitive platform allows easy navigation and management with due dates, notes, projects, and tasks.

Toontastic by Launchpad Toys (Free)

Digital storytelling for younger students is fun and engaging with this app. Users draw and animate their own cartoons, and can choose from several situational settings to describe mood, feelings, and themes. This app can be used as a first tool and introduction to stories and storytelling.

TOTALe HD by Rosetta Stone (Free for Rosetta Stone subscribers)

TOTALe HD allows users to continue Rosetta Stone language lessons on the go, and the iPad app allows full access to the same curriculum and activities as the program through the computer. Mobile devices other than the iPad allow for review but are limited in the lessons and activities features of the program.

TV Guide by TV Guide (Free)

You will know that you've made the transition to mobile devices when you use your handheld device to search TV listings. This app also allows users to set up reminders for favorite small-screen shows and to manage channels. The feature that provides breaking entertainment news is helpful when looking for pop culture topics to integrate into a library program.

Twitter by Twitter, Inc. (Free)

Twitter's official iPad app has a great interface that you might like better than the website on your computer. There is much less clutter, and all the tools you need—including Mentions, Messages, Lists, Profile, Search, and the Timeline—are available. Twitter, when used as a professional development tool and a medium for sharing information with your patrons, might just be the justification to have open access at your school.

Virtuoso Piano Free 2 HD by Peterb (Free)

Play or learn to play the piano on this free instrument. If you need more features than the free app provides, you can upgrade to the premium app.

The Weather Channel by The Weather Channel Interactive (Free)

This app can be used for personal interest as well as in the classroom. Students will develop stronger interest and understanding of global issues when they have a deeper knowledge of how weather relates to events or places. Interactive interfaces and imagery add to the experience and will engage students.

WebMD for iPad by WebMD (Free)

The healthcare app's content from the WebMD Health Network includes WebMD Health, Medscape, MedicineNet, EMedicineHealth, RxList, TheHeart.org, Drugs.com, and Medscape Education. The disclaimer on the app reminds users that it should not be used for diagnosis and treatment, an important statement that might lead a classroom discussion regarding media and information literacy. First Aid information is available through the app without a wi-fi or 3G network connection, and the drugs and treatments feature, along with the symptom checker and local health listings, make this a good mobile health care partner.

Wikipanion for iPad by Robert Chin (Free)

Wikipedia entries come up early in every Google search, but this app makes searching and using Wikipedia so much easier and faster. Lots of features such as interactive font resizing, full in-page searching, and image saving to the photo library are included. Although most of us have been programmed to deny that any reliable information can be gleaned from Wikipedia, recent improvements within the organization and website have made the source so much more reliable and useful for at least popular culture and personal interest topics. Wikipedia and Wikipanion are terrific topics for media literacy discussions about the impact and use of social media and crowd sourced information.

Wordfoto by bitCycle AB ($)

This might be one of the most popular photo editor apps today. It is unique in that it creates typographic images from photos, which means that the words you add or choose are embedded into the photo. Features include captions for the photos, cropping, and quite a few fine-tuning features. This photo-blending tool takes word clouds one step further. Students can transform their own photos with both informative and dramatic results to use in presentations or assignments.

WolframAlpha by Wolfram Alpha LLC ($)

A huge collection of algorithms and data will compute and answer just about any question or problem. Topics covered in the app include math, statistics, astronomy, chemistry, physics, engineering, dates and times, and more. And here's a bit of trivia to know: the iPhone's assistant, Siri, uses the WolframAlpha algorithms to respond to users' needs.

World Atlas HD by National Geographic Society ($)

World flags, high-resolution maps, and global facts are available to bookmark and create notes. A single finger tap on the iPad accesses the 3D globe and facts. This app is a dynamic tool that might just replace those quickly outdated print books and resources in the library.

XE Currency for iPad by EX.com, Inc. (Free)

Some reviewers have described this currency convertor as ugly or unattractive. Maybe I don't expect enough from this app, or currency convertors in general, but it converts everything I need it to very well. It's simple to use and has many features that can be set according to individual preferences. I believe the app will come in handy when students study global issues, countries, and cultures.

YALSA's Teen Book Finder by The American Library Association (Free)

Looking for a YA or teen book can't be any easier than using this free app developed by the Young Adult Library Services Association (YALSA). Educators from across the country have selected the books in the finder. Both hot picks of the day and a search menu with options such as search by titles, author, genre, year, award, and booklist are available. Collection development, personal use, and classroom assignments are potential uses. The app was developed for the iPhone and iPod Touch, so the screen is small on the iPad.

Zillow Real Estate: Homes and Apartments, for Sale or Rent by Zillow.com (Free)

Home values, tax history, a mortgage calculator, and a GPS can become tools for students to study economic issues regarding the housing industry. For personal use, Zillow is a great tool to keep an eye on your own neighborhood's market values or to find homes for sale or rent.

Zite by Zite, Inc. (Free)

Similar in purpose to Flipboard, this iPad newsreader or aggregator defines itself as your personal magazine. It uses your Twitter and Google Reader accounts to draw content, and it has a very readable format that reflects a newspaper or magazine.

APP DIRECTORIES

Appitic is a directory of more than 1,800 apps for education by Apple Distinguished Educators (ADEs). The directory makes navigation and browsing very easy with the drop-down menus that reveal subjects and categories of any topic or field that you can imagine within education. For example, art, patterns, math, Spanish, German, language arts, tools, thinking skills, science, reference, music, and social studies include either broader or narrower topics, and, there are additional subjects for special education, multiple intelligences, Bloom's taxonomy, and teacher resources. Reviews, cost, and the objectives of each recommended app are provided through the Appitic website.

Another directory that boasts 50,000 of the best educational apps, and provides comparison charts and information is a website created through a

partnership between Edudemic.com and FindTheBest.com (http://apps
.edudemic.com). The recommended apps list does contain many popular apps
for all levels of education (from preschool to university levels), but it is a
long, robust list that is global in scope. Many apps on the list are intended for
countries beyond the United States. If you are looking for an app in French,
Finnish, or for a very specific purpose, this app directory will be useful. And
the nicely designed search feature allows users to search by grade level, app
price, intended device, or operating system.

Our school preloads and pushes out teacher-chosen apps to students' iPads for
use in the classroom, but we also allow students to upload apps that they desire
and wish to purchase themselves. Since iPads and mobile devices are designed
as personal tools, and our goal is to develop tech-agile students, the decision was
made to allow individuals the ability to make choices and determine personal
needs. To do otherwise would be counterproductive in our educational setting.

Hopefully, you will become a reviewer and chooser of apps for your school.
Create or suggest the formation of a committee that is charged with finding,
reviewing, compiling, and determining which common apps will be installed
on every student's iPad. As the school librarian or media specialist, it's important that you join or create that group for your school. Talk with the early adopters and teens who are reliable sources for the newest scoop; keep your ear to the
ground and help spread the word for the apps just as you would for any other
useful educational or personal resource.

LIBRARY APPS

I mentioned earlier how our library catalog app is my current favorite app. The
app, created for our library management system, is compatible with Android,
iPhone, and iPod Touch devices. Here are some of the functions that I am learning I can't live without:

- Barcode scanning using iPhone and Android phones' camera function. When
  I see a book in a bookstore, at the grocery, or on my friend's kitchen counter,
  I can just scan the barcode to see if it's available in my library, public library,
  or my regular bookseller's site or store to compare prices and availability.
- Accessing all libraries, not just our school library, which use the same library
  management system is an option that comes in handy when I'm searching for
  a specific title for a patron and might want to request an ILL.
- The app can be customized and fully branded for our school and library. Our
  small and modest collection now looks as attractive and robust as the biggest
  and best library systems and booksellers.
- Students can check their accounts (with my permission and settings) and
  place their own holds on items.
- So much is customizable, and today's options are only the beginning.

Publishers and vendors are working hard to develop and introduce apps for their databases, eBooks, and other sources of information. These apps offer quick access to the information specific to that company. That's good news and bad news. The good news is that students and patrons have constant and mobile access to reliable information. The bad news is that students like one-stop shopping, and they are not as likely to switch back and forth among apps to find the right and appropriate information for a specific need. To help students organize and keep library resources visible and available, suggest to students that they cluster their library and research-related apps together in a single folder. That will work as a visual and spatial reminder that these apps are related.

In addition to creating a suggested or recommended app directory for your community, add suggested or recommended apps to research pathfinders and guides that you create for specific classroom assignments and projects.

If you are like most new iPad or tablet users, you'll find that initially it's difficult to push that install button for an app, but once you discover that it's just as easy to delete it if you change your mind, it becomes easier, and finally, easy. One of the biggest advantages that you can provide to your school community is to become the app finder, recommender, and curator so that all students using mobile devices will have what they need for specific purposes or interests.

7

Discover Your Favorite Power Tools

This final chapter offers the tools that you need to help you step outside of your comfort zone and experiment, create, and reinvent your library program. The following annotated lists include recommended media tools, superheroes of our profession, pop culture sources, and the traditional professional development resources that librarians have used for decades, but now, with additional online features.

Experiment with these media tools and use them, share with teachers, and teach students how to integrate them into their classroom activities and assignments. Discover your favorite websites and pop culture sources, and use today's current news, trends, and trivia to interact and connect with students in order to make learning more relevant for them. Study the list of our profession's leaders, who offer the newest trends and professional advice. Then run—don't walk—to subscribe, follow, and watch these superheroes. Use the final list to amplify professional development resources that you likely already use and develop a healthy obsession to regularly connect to the additional online features that present the most timely and up-to-date resources available.

It's never been easier to keep up with library and education trends and leaders in our profession; social media makes it simple to stay connected and aware. Twitter handles, blog URLs, Facebook and LinkedIn pages, websites, and other information is included in the lists so that you can easily follow your favorite superheroes and read their updates that are pushed to you without any additional seeking, searching, or bookmarking.

Examine the following tools that I am recommending (in alphabetical order) and consider a close examination of those that pique your curiosity. Tools and concepts come and go, and it is up to each educator and librarian to seek out, discover, and use what works best for them and their students. Find those that work for you and begin to recharge your library program.

MEDIA TOOLS

These following media tools are either just emerging or have already become some of the most popular tools for students and teachers. Because so many fall into several categories, I've place them in alphabetical order for easy access.

Animoto

URL: http://www.animoto.com
Twitter: @Animoto

About the Program: This video creator uses photos, videos, text, and music to create wow-worthy videos. Animoto is constantly adding new features and tools to keep it fresh and new, and the program is easy enough for very young students to manage, and for older students to create in-depth presentations. Consider promoting its use for presentations, class assignments, webpage welcomes, or for biographical video shows. Or use it to entertain at open houses, assemblies, weddings, birthdays, or anniversaries. Educational accounts are available for teachers for free, and students can sign up through their teacher's account for free access as well.

Bag the Web

URL: www.bagtheweb.com

About the Program: Organize your favorite websites and social media with this free tool. There are worthwhile tutorials and simple steps for creating "bags" of information by topic or category. Keep your bags private or share them with students, teachers, colleagues, and your social media followers through Twitter, LinkedIn, and Facebook. Add and use the bookmarklet (quick method of adding sites to your bag) in your tool bar, iPhone, or iPad. The bags you create can also be embedded into the research pathfinders or guides that you create for students.

Beeclip.edu

URL: http://www.beeclip.com/

About the Program: Beeclip.edu is an education friendly version of Beeclip. Teachers can manage their classes and projects, and students use the management feature. Like Beeclip, this program allows users to tell their stories through scrapbooks, collages, posters, portfolios, and mood boards. I used this with young students, seven through 12-year-olds. They needed little instruction and guidance, and they loved the stickers and templates provided. Best yet, the program is free, there is nothing to download, and projects can be shared or kept private.

Big Huge Labs

URL: http://www.bighugelabs.com/

About the Program: Big Huge Labs is correctly titled. It's a huge site full of creativity labs that utilize photos, images, and text. For example, students can create personalized magazine covers, movie posters, mosaics, and trading cards with their own photos that they upload. I've used the movie poster creator with students, and I have been happily surprised with their enthusiasm and enjoyment of the project. This site is ideal for making book display posters to grab students' and patrons' attention.

Blockposters

URL: http://www.blockposters.com/

About the Program: Use Blockposters to create any size wall posters from any uploaded images and print them from your regular and everyday color printer. There is nothing to download, and the service is free. The process is simple: upload an image, choose the size and number of individual sheets of paper you want or need, save, print, and trim and tape the pieces together. This is an easy and inexpensive way to create personalized posters with students and teachers as the stars.

Blurb

URL: http://lp.blurb.com/
Twitter: @BlurbBooks

About the Website: This website is truly an online publishing program. Whether you, teachers, or your students want to create photo books, scrapbooks, or a great American novel, this tool will do it for you with high-quality paper, binding, and layout. One of the best features is that you can convert your book to an iPad or iPhone format with the typical two-page layout with high-resolution images, and readers have the ability to zoom in and out. In addition, books can be sold through Blurb.com.

Brainshark

URL: http://www.brainshark.com/
Twitter: Brainshark

About the Program: Brainshark's basic program is free (single user), and this level might be all that you need to create some very slick and professional presentations. You can upload PowerPoint slides, documents, photos, and more, and enhance them with voice narration. You can also share your presentations through social media, e-mail, or an app on your mobile device.

Bundlr

URL: http://bundlr.com/
Twitter: @Bundlr

About the Program: Bundlr is a social information-gathering site that allows users to create "bundles" of web information by category or topic. This easy-to-use program helps you organize articles, photos, websites, videos, and social media posts. The free program is accessible through a Google profile, Facebook, or Twitter account. Students might find it useful for creating bundles of information for projects, and collaboration among users is permitted and encouraged. However, there is no method of adding articles directly from proprietary databases or uploading images and photos. I like the appearance of a bundle with a choice of a list or chart view, and each user can choose his or her preferred style.

Collaborize Classroom

URL: http://www.collaborizeclassroom.com/

About the Program: This robust cloud program is free and has many of the same features as expensive classroom management software programs. Students and teachers can meet online to discuss or respond to prompts or questions, and teachers can share resources and documents with students. In addition, the Collaborize Classroom Topic Library is an online community of teachers who share lesson plans, ideas, and methods.

Comicmaster

URL: http://www.comicmaster.org.uk/

About the Program: Students of any age absolutely love this cartoon and graphic novel creator. Users create stories with colorful images, props, backgrounds, special effects, and more. Many choices are offered for the formatting of each page and adding dialogue or captions to bring the images to life. This tool is valuable for digital storytelling as well as reluctant readers or writers. The program is free but requires registration in order to save work and have it available at a later date. However, users can print and take a screen shot without registration.

Corkboardme

URL: http://corkboard.me/

About the Program: The Corkboardme website is so colorful and cheerful that students will love sharing notes for classroom projects and collaborations. There are many uses for this program, but it can be easily used as a brainstorming, note taking, or task tool. A free and new corkboard is available each time you go to the website. However, for power users, an upgraded Pro level with many more features is available.

Flixtime

URL: http://flixtime.com/

About the Program: This video creation program takes users' photos, text, videos, and music, and turns them into high-energy videos. Accounts are free, and students can add their own photos, videos, and music or choose from Flixtime's library. Free accounts limit videos to 60 seconds in length, but upgrades for longer videos and more features are available.

GameStar

URL: http://gamestarmechanic.com/

About the Program: This video game creator might be just what teachers who want to teach students how to think critically, understand elements of design and aesthetics, and problem solve, need to get started. A basic free program will provide some fun for students, but the upgraded robust program with its many features and facets becomes a serious educational tool that will engage any student, young or old.

Glogster

URL: http://glogster.com/
Twitter: @Glogster or @GlogsterEDU

About the Website: Glogster is a free social media expression tool. Users can mash photos, text, videos, and audio; add special effects into digital posters, collages, or scrapbooks. The educational site http://edu.glogster.com offers classroom and student management tools on a private and secure platform. However, the education site is not free. Check out the website to see the several levels of service and pricing that are available to educators.

Go Animate

URL: http://goanimate.com/

About the Program: This program has so much potential for engaging students and teachers, and it can be used for so many things like creative writing, tutorials, class assignments and presentations, foreign language review, and demos. Go Animate is a video creation program that uses animated, cartoon-type characters that users choose. Students or educators narrate the video to explain, teach, describe, and tell. This tool isn't inexpensive, but there is educational pricing that might just make it irresistible. Also, a free trial is available.

Goodreads

URL: http://www.goodreads.com/
Twitter: @Goodreads

About the Program: I am so excited about this website. It's never been easier to keep lists of what you've read, want to read, and are currently reading. And you can quickly write a review or comment so that your friends and followers might be advised accordingly. Start an account for your school library and feed recommended books to it to share with teachers and students. Have students create their own accounts and lists, and form or join a book club. Goodreads provides additional features such as trivia, recommendations, quizzes, quotes, and more. There is also an app for keeping up with your account on the go.

HelloSlide

URL: http://www.helloslide.com/

About the Program: Take your PowerPoint slides in PDF format, or any documents you want to use; write a description, speech, or explanation for each slide; and allow HelloSlide to create a computer-generated narrated presentation for you. Foreign language teachers will love the feature that allows users to choose from a list of languages for the narration. Create a presentation and post it on your website to use as a tutorial or demo. A basic program is free, and if you want to upgrade, education accounts are discounted. For those users not ready to star in their own video, narration, or screen recording, this program will fill the gap. And it's so easy to use.

Hootsuite

URL: http://hootsuite.com/
Twitter: @Hootsuite

About the Program: Hootsuite manages all your social media accounts so that you don't need to watch each one individually. The free account allows up to five social networking accounts and two Atom/RSS feeds, provides reports, and allows you to schedule messages to be posted. There is a free level of service with an option to try out the upgraded levels before committing.

Inanimate Alice

URL: http://www.inanimatealice.com/
Twitter: @InanimateAlice

About the Program: This program is truly an original digital novel that is both unique and interactive. Created in an electronic format, Inanimate Alice uses text, images, music, sound effects, puzzles, and games to illustrate and enhance the narrative. It is a program that will entice even the most reluctant readers and writers to become engaged. Teacher resources that include an introduction, education pack, and a starter activities booklet are available in addition to information for parents.

Issuu

URL: http://issuu.com/
Twitter: @Issuu

About the Program: This digital publishing site turns your PDF documents into digital presentations. Save any document or presentation as a PDF file and upload it to Issuu to see how it morphs into a bright and shiny digital document. Ideas for using Issuu include library reports, library brochures and documents for recruitment purposes, library user or policy manuals, and newsletters. You can share the publications by e-mail or embed them into your webpage.

Jing

URL: http://www.techsmith.com/jing

About the Program: Jing is a free and simple to use screen recorder for videos and images. It is a Techsmith program and the younger sibling of Camtasia, a screen recorder with editing features. Techsmith pays attention to details and makes navigation easy for new users, even with the free Jing program. Even though Jing doesn't allow editing and limits recordings to five minutes or less, it functions beautifully for quick and dirty instruction in a flipped classroom setting, tutorials for patrons on how to use your catalog or databases, or an introduction to your library and library website. I usually write a script and read from it as I navigate and record a presentation of websites and information.

Jux

URL: https://jux.com/

About the Program: Jux is wall-to-wall gorgeous. This free graphic blog fills the entire screen with your images and information, displaying them in high resolution. Students can tell stories through images and add captions or text. This site is ideal for digital storytelling and information collages. A picture really does paint a thousand words in this program. Posts can be shared through social media.

Kids' Magnetic Poetry Kit

URL: http://play.magpogames.com/poem/Kids/kit/

About the Program: Even students who hate writing will find this free program fun and engaging. As soon as you link to the site, the fun begins. Words appear on the page, and users drag them to create phrases, sentences, poems, or stories. Add more words with a simple click of a button and share the work through e-mail or social media. It's a great tool to learn new vocabulary, introduce creative writing, or motivate reluctant writers.

Knovio

URL: http://www.knovio.com
Twitter: @Knovio

About the Program: Your trusty PowerPoint slides, a web cam, and a microphone (both usually built into your laptop or computer) are all you need to create video tutorials, demos, or presentations that you can e-mail, post on your webpage, or share through social media. This tool really takes something very basic and turns it into a tool that will connect with students.

Linkbunch

URL: http://www.linkbun.ch/

About the Program: Linkbunch is a website aggregator that allows you to create "bunches" of information to share with others through e-mail or social media. The beauty of this web organizer is that the link that you share is an abbreviated URL that links to a page with your website links. This is a clean and tidy tool for those who hate clutter.

LULU

URL: http://www.lulu.com/

About the Program: This online publisher allows individuals to self-publish an eBook or print book and to sell it online through the major online booksellers such as Barnes & Noble, Amazon, and iBookstore. LULU will handle as much or as little as you would like. Editing, printing, cover design, marketing, formatting, reviews, and more are offered. LULU also provides tools for publishing poetry books, photo books, cookbooks, calendars, and more. Share this online tool with teachers so that they can integrate the study of publishing through students' creative writing or storytelling assignments.

Make Believe Comics

URL: http://www.makebeliefscomix.com/

About the Program: There are infinite uses for this comic-making program in a school setting. Make Believe Comics can be used for digital storytelling, student reports about people or events, creative writing, motivating reluctant writers and readers, and more. I've used this program with students from ages seven to 12, and every student was enthusiastic about it. In his blog that is linked form the site, the creator—Bill Zimmerman—provides writing prompts and ideas for incorporating Make Believe Comics into the curriculum.

MentorMob

URL: http://www.mentormob.com/
Twitter: @MentorMob

About the Program: This program might be the most exciting new product for sharing information, skills, tools, and links. I'm planning to incorporate it into my media literacy instruction this school year. MentorMob allows users to create visual playlists from websites, documents, photos, and articles. It also provides a quiz tool to check your target audience's knowledge. Easy-to-use tutorials and demos will walk you through the process of creating your own playlists. Tell your teachers and students about this tool—it's unique and robust.

Meograph

URL: http://www.meograph.com/
Twitter: @Meograph

About the Program: Meograph is a storytelling tool that incorporates maps, timelines, video, images and photos, voice recordings, and links to information or websites. Students can use Meograph as a presentation tool for a class assignment about current events, history, interviews or personal storytelling, and more. For example, Charles Darwin's life and discoveries could be presented by taking the audience on a visual journey to his birthplace, young life highlights, important events and breakthroughs, and articles and biographical information. Results can be shared through social media. View the demos and let yourself imagine ways this tool can be incorporated into your school.

Mightybell

URL: http://mightybell.com/

About the Program: This online social media program allows individuals and groups to work together to solve a problem, create a project, or discuss ideas and issues. Although not originally designed for education, the tool would work well for any collaborative project with students or teachers. Add a website link, and the site appears as a page. Add text, questions, photos, documents, and more.

My Storymaker

URL: http://www.clpgh.org/kids/storymaker/embed.cfm

About the Program: This digital storytelling program provides animated characters, page formats, backgrounds and settings, and dialogue balloons in which young students can create stories. This could be used for students' very first storytelling or creative writing project. The steps are simple and intuitive.

Paper.li

URL: http://paper.li/
Twitter: @SmallRivers

About the Program: Paper.li is a content curation service that pulls information from social media sites to display, organize, and highlight your newest and most relevant posts. I've been using Paper.li with my school library's Twitter account, and when I tweet my newly released issue, it looks like I've spent hours, days, or weeks to create it. Images, headlines, and features will engage your followers. You can set your own schedule for creating issues and then just forget about it. The newest issue will be pushed to you, and you can choose when and how to post it.

Pinterest

URL: http://pinterest.com/
Twitter: @Pinterest

About the Site: The fact that Pinterest has become so popular with users of all ages confirms how easy and useful it is. The program is a web pinboard, or bulletin board, that encourages users to find and post images from websites. To satisfy users' diverse interests, many new boards may be added to an account. Classroom or library uses might include current events boards, political campaign boards, book titles, genres, or themes and trivia from any subject area. I recommend creating a separate account for your school and professional life.

Present.me

URL: http://present.me/

About the Program: Show, tell, and share is the mantra of Present.me. Upload existing PPT, PDF, DOC and other file formats, and turn them into a narrated video. There is no learning curve. This is the easiest video creation program I've discovered—I created a successful test presentation without even watching a demo or tutorial. This program will work well as a tutorial or as a tool for students to review material when you post it online. The free program is generous in allowing three presentations a month, 15 minutes per presentation, and one private presentation per month. Also, they offer discounts for education accounts.

Prezi

URL: http://prezi.com/
Twitter: @Prezi

About the Program: It's obvious why Prezi has become so popular. It takes all the features that we rely on from other slide and presentation tools and makes the presentation feel more natural and comfortable. Images, text, videos, and audio seem so much brighter when viewed from the Prezi pathway. Users can manipulate the show by zooming in and out to emphasize information, and by controlling the pace and rhythm. The free iPad app for Prezi allows editing, and the pinch screen feature makes presenting simple. There is an incline on the learning curve for Prezi, but the tutorials and help tools are great. Students love Prezi and usually choose it when creating a presentation for a class, club, or school.

QR Codes

About the Media: QR codes are everywhere in today's world. In retail shop windows, on "for sale" signs in front of houses, in newspaper ads, and more. I've been putting a QR code on our patron library cards for a few years, and the code takes users to our library's website. I've used QR codes with young students in summer programs and have students use the text feature to describe themselves. There are many, many websites that offer educational uses and ideas for QR codes. Ideas include scavenger hunts, voting and polling, poetry, and writing prompts.

Kayway http://qrcode.kaywa.com/
QRstuff http://www.qrstuff.com/
Goqr.me http://goqr.me/

Redux

URL: http://redux.com/

About the Program: Redux makes your laptop, computer—and soon tablet—into a television device for video. Redux curators are searching constantly from sources like ESPN, YouTube, and Vimeo for videos within popular categories such as daily news, human interest, medical help, counterculture, and more. I watched a National Geographic HD video about safaris, and the resolution along with wall-to-wall image makes it comparable to watching on an HD TV. Teachers will love having a collection of high-quality videos available for classes to view.

Scoop.it

URL: http://www.scoop.it/
Twitter: @Scoopit

About the Program: This web curation tool takes content that users choose themselves and turns it into glossy, high-resolution graphic publications. For example, a teacher might create a Scoop.it publication on the topic of gentrification, providing images, maps, photos, blog posts, and articles about different viewpoints on the topic. The result is visual and certain to be something students will want to read. Specific posts can be "rescooped" and posted to social media. A downloadable bookmarklet makes scooping web content fast and easy. This tool would also make a great scrapbooking or digital storytelling tool for the classroom.

Screencast-O-matic

URL: http://screencast-o-matic.com/

About the Program: This free screen recorder offers a longer recording time (15 minutes per video) than most free accounts from other screen recorder programs. And you can allow your finished product to be hosted by Screencast-o-matic or publish to YouTube, MP4, AVI, or FLV movie. I've used this product many times to record tutorials for our students. There are no editing features in the free program, but if you have a script and practice once or twice, you should be able to go through your recording without needing to edit. The more often you create screen recordings, the more efficient you will become. If you want to upgrade to a level with editing and other features, you can do so at a low annual cost. Screencast-o-matic is easy, and the results are good-quality videos that you can post for your patrons.

SlideRocket

URL: http://www.sliderocket.com/
Twitter: @SlideRocket

About the Program: SlideRocket is a slide presentation program that makes slide presentations fresh and new. The transitions, formats, layouts, and templates are all familiar yet refreshed. If you prefer slide shows to video or audio media, you need to check out SlideRocket. Although this program is targeted to business and the consumer marketplace, there is a free account available, and educators will find the features perfect for classroom and professional use.

Storify

URL: http://storify.com/

About the Program: Storify is a web curation tool that allows users to pull specific information from social media posts and websites, to share. A bookmarklet is available to make choosing information simple and easy. Storify turns the chosen information into a narrative. Images, headlines, blog posts, videos, and more become an overview of a topic, and the creator can write his or her own narration, comments, text, and headlines within the story. This tool would be useful for current issue topics in the classroom or for digital storytelling projects.

Tagxedo

URL: http://www.tagxedo.com/
Twitter: @Tagxedo

About the Program: Tagxedo is a word cloud creator, and as with other cloud creator programs, users type, paste blocks of text, or choose a website to insert words. The words then become an art design based on selected fonts, colors, and styles. Tagxedo steps the word cloud world up a notch by allowing users to choose a shape for the cloud. A speech by Lincoln celebrating President's Day might appear in a word cloud defined by the shape of Lincoln's distinctive head. Another word cloud might be comprised of words of a poem and the shape defined by a tree, bird, or heart. Tagxedo might just be the tool to motivate reluctant readers and writers to engage with words. And it's great to create an image for a presentation or display, or as a first or last slide of a presentation. There is a small download needed to use Tagxedo.

Tinkercad

URL: https://tinkercad.com/home/
Twitter: @Tinkercad

About the Program: This computer-aided design (CAD) design program works as a useful introduction to 3D design. Both young and older students will immediately begin playing with the tools that Tinkercad provides on its homepage. The basic program is free, and the tutorials and demos will make designers out of the most timid students. I used this program with young students during a summer camp, and they were teaching features to each other in just a few minutes.

Tumblr

URL: http://www.tumblr.com/
Twitter: @Tumblr

About the Program: This blog program has both an iPhone and an Android app as well as a dashboard widget for Mac bloggers that makes it a mobile and easy-to-use program. Tumblr has features that include inserting video, text, links, photos, and images, and it is easy to use with quite a few customization features and templates for free. To make choosing what you want to post easy and fast, a bookmarklet is available for Tumblr.

Vialogues

URL: http://vialogues.com/
Twitter: @Vialogues

About the Program: Students watch videos to expand their knowledge about a topic and to reinforce understanding in the classroom. Teachers constantly use videos as educational tools. Vialogues allows videos to become the center of learning rather than an addition. Educators post a video, participants watch it, and everyone joins in a discussion about it. The discussion can be recorded and archived for grading purposes or for later use.

Wordle

URL: http://www.wordle.net/

About the Program: Wordle is the original word cloud generator. It creates images from words or text that the user provides. The text is then transformed into designs, and the user can modify colors, fonts, and styles. Students will find studying about a speech, poem, or prose more engaging when they can transform the text into a personally designed word cloud. There is nothing to download—the fun begins as soon you link to the website.

Zamzar

URL: http://www.zamzar.com/

About the Program: Have you ever gotten the error messages Unrecognized File Type or Wrong File Type? Confused about what to do or what it means for you? Zamzar is here to rescue you. The free file conversion program will help transform music, video, images, and documents into the format you need.

You can even convert a file format straight from e-mail. This is a handy book-mark to have ready when the need arises.

POP CULTURE

Use pop culture to connect with teens and other students; create media, infor-mation, technology, or transliteracy instruction; display popular movies, books, celebrity news, and events; or create programs that incorporate current news and events. Do whatever works for you that will keep library resources and services relevant and interesting to teens and other students. Keep an eye on the pop culture horizon by scanning topics, people, events, and news from the following information sources.

Alexander Russo's Blog, This Week in Education

Affiliation: Scholastic
URL: http://scholasticadministrator.typepad.com/thisweekineducation/school_life_/
Author: Alexander Russo
Twitter: @alexanderrusso
Facebook: http://www.facebook.com/alexanderrusso
Pinterest: http://pinterest.com/hotfored/hot-for-education-2012/

About the Blog: What is different about Russo's pop culture blog is that it mixes pop culture news with educational issues at the policymaking level. For example, a post about the school in which Suri Cruise is now enrolled for a mere $40,000 a year is followed by a post a week later about gender balance for cam-paign debate moderators. Russo is a former Senate staffer, and his interest in poli-tics related to to education is evident in most of his posts. There are so many reasons to follow Russo and his posts, but here are a few of the primary ones: read-ers will stay up to date with issues surrounding education and politics, educators can adopt his pop culture topics for research topics that will make students think critically about important issues that affect them as students, and the news, videos, TV shows, and movies that relate to schools, students, and teachers will make you the hippest faculty member at the lunch table.

Connect the Pop: At the Intersection of Pop Culture, Transliteracy, and Critical Thinking

Affiliation: *School Library Journal (SLJ)*
URL: http://blogs.slj.com/connect-the-pop/
Author: Peter Gutierrez
E-mail: fiifgutierrez@gmail.com

LinkedIn: petergutierrez
Twitter: @Peter_Gutierrez

About the Blog: This SLJ blog is so much more than just pop culture news and information. Gutierrez is a former teacher, current writer, and media literacy specialist, and the blog offers educational methods and tips for using pop culture to engage students through the classroom.

New York Times (NYT), The Learning Network Blog: Teaching and Learning with the New York Times

Affiliation: The *New York Times*
URL: http://learning.blogs.nytimes.com/category/lesson-plans/media-studies/popular-culture/
Twitter: @NYTlearning

About the Blog: This *NYT* blog falls under the Education category, and it is a direct connection to pop culture events and information. In addition, many lesson plans based on the *NYT*'s content, contests, critical thinking questions, daily crossword, and vocabulary words for students are offered for free. The free resources include the following topics: American History, Civics, Current Events, Economics, Fine Arts, Geography, Global History, Health, Journalism, Language Arts, Mathematics, Media Studies, Science, Social Studies, Technology, and Academic Skills. Students 13 years of age and older are encouraged to comment online to current issues involving the news.

NPR Arts and Life: Pop Culture

Affiliation: NPR
URL: http://www.npr.org/sections/pop-culture/

About the Website: This blog focuses on pop culture in television, digital life, and media. Images, audio stories, and podcasts related to specific topics are available.

Pop Culture Madness

Affiliation: PCM Networks
URL: http://www.popculturemadness.com/
Twitter: @PCMTweet

About the Blog: This is one of the most comprehensive pop culture websites you'll find, and along with the latest celebrity gossip, entertainment news, and events, there is trivia for each month, pop music listed from each decade, and information about film, DVD, music, and television. This is an easy-to-use site that provides a lot of facts and news quickly.

Pop Culture Universe by ABC-CLIO

Affiliation: ABC-CLIO
URL: http://www.abc-clio.com/product.aspx?id=2147488617
ISBN: 978-1-59884-559-4

About the Resource: Most teachers understand the importance of creating assignments that relate to students' interests and lives, and this database will be a necessity in your library collection in your quest solve those information needs. When your students need an authoritative source for studying history and for their pop culture research project, you will likely find everything they need in *Pop Culture Universe*. Topics covering the past and present will satisfy a variety of research interests and needs, and the photos, articles, and topic overviews will engage young researchers.

SUPERHEROES

Become your superhero, avatar or alter ego and rescue your library program.

Frank Baker

Blog: Frequent blogger for *USA Today*'s The Teachers' Lounge
URL: http://www.usatodayeducation/teacherslounge
Website: Media Literacy Clearinghouse
URL: http://www.frankwbaker.com
E-mail: FBaker1346@aol.com
Twitter: @fbaker
Facebook: http://www.facebook.com/medialiteracyman
Books and Publications:

- *Media Literacy in the K-12 Classroom*. International Society for Technology in Education (ISTE), 2012.
- *Political Campaigns and Political Advertising: A Media Literacy Guide*. Greenwood, 2009.
- *Coming Distractions: Questioning Movies* (Media Literacy series). Capstone Press, 2007.

About His Posts: Baker is an expert on media literacy and works as a consultant and presenter around the world to educate teachers and school administrators about the importance of media literacy. His posts on *USA Today*'s Teachers' Lounge recognize library media specialists' essential role in creating media-savvy students who will continue to think critically about the world around them beyond our school walls. His books should be in every professional collection, and his ideas should be among those discussed with teachers in every professional learning network.

Richard Byrne

Blog: Free Technology for Teachers
URL: http://www.freetech4teachers.com/
E-mail: richardbyrne@freetech4teachers.com
Twitter: @rmbyrne

About the Blog: Byrne focuses on free resources that educators can use as classroom tools, and he creates and writes many of the resources that he provides on his blog. Free and available downloadable documents by Byrne that you can get straight from his website include:

* Ten Digital Storytelling Projects
* How to do 11 Techy Things in the Next School Year
* Google for Teachers: Books, Docs, Maps, and More
* Google for Teachers II
* Google Earth Across the Curriculum
* Beyond Google: Tips and Tricks for Improving Internet Search Experiences
* Twelve Essentials for Technology Integration
* Making Videos on the Web: Make videos without purchasing software or video equipment

Awards:

* Edublog, Best Ed Tech Blog 2011, 2011
* Edublog, Best Individual Blog 2009, 2010
* Edublog, Best Ed Tech Support Blog 2010
* Edublog, awards for Best Resource Sharing Blog 2008, 2009, 2010

Michael Gorman

Blog: 21st Century Educational Technology and Learning
URL: http://21centuryedtech.wordpress.com/
Twitter: @mjgormans

About the Blog: Gorman, author of the 21st Century Educational Technology and Learning blog, advocates for and provides an endless amount of free resources for teachers, students, and school librarians. Gorman's goal of engaging students to enhance learning is constantly a presence throughout his posts. Topics discussed in the blog include technology, teaching and learning methods, twenty-first-century skills, Science, Technology, Engineering, and Mathematics (STEM) education, and project-based learning.

Awards:

- Top 40 Most Trusted Educational Blog
- Top 50 Education Innovator
- Star Discovery Educator
- Top 100 Education Blog by Online Degrees.org

Buffy Hamilton

Blog: The Unquiet Librarian
URL: http://theunquietlibrarian.wordpress.com/
Website: http://buffyjhamilton.wordpress.com/
E-mail:

- buffy.hamilton@cpl.org
- buffy.hamilton@gmail.com

Twitter: @buffyjhamilton
Books and Publications:

- *Embedded Librarianship: Tools and Practices*, ALA TechSource. 2012.
- "Give Them Something to Talk About: The Kindle Pilot Program at the Unquiet Library," in *No Shelf Required 2: Use and Management of Electronic Books*, S. Polanka, ed., Chicago: ALA Editions, 2012.
- "Embedded Librarianship: A High School Case Study," in *E-Reference Context and Discoverability in Libraries: Issues and Concepts*, S. Polanka, ed., Hershey, PA: IGI Global, 2011.
- "School," in *The Atlas of New Librarianship*, R.D. Lankes, ed., Cambridge, MA: MIT Press, 2011.
- "The School Librarian as Teacher: What Kind of Teacher Are You?" *Knowledge Quest* 39, no. 9 (2011): 34–40.
- "Creating Conversations for Learning: School Libraries as Sites of Participatory Culture," *School Library Monthly*, 27, no. 8 (2011): 41.
- "Pivots for Change: Libraries and Librarians," *Library Media Connection*, 2010.
- "Young Adult Literature 2.0," *Library Media Connection*, 2009.
- "Poetry Goes 2.0," *Library Media Connection*, 2009.
- "Transforming Information Literacy for Nowgen Students," *Knowledge Quest*, 2009.

About the Blog: Hamilton's voice is strong, clear, and vibrant in the school library world, and she brings the most current and relevant trends and topics to blogs and Twitter feeds. For example, eBook platforms, transliteracy, participatory school cultures, and social media are part of her repertoire, and she is constant and consistent in her postings.

Awards:

- *Library Journal*'s Movers and Shakers 2011
- Salem Press Best School Library Blog 2011
- American Library Association (ALA) Office for Information Technology Policy (OITP) Cutting Edge Library Service Award
- Georgia Library Media Association/Georgia Association for Instructional Technology School Library Media Specialist of the Year 2010–11
- National School Boards Association Technology Leadership Network "20 to Watch" 2010
- Tech and Learning's 100@30: Future Leader
- Georgia Exemplary High School Media Program 2010
- GLMA North Central Georgia District Media Specialist of the Year 2010
- Teacher of the Year Finalist, Creekview High School 2010
- Edublog, Nominee for Best Library/Librarian Blog 2009
- Teacher of the Year Finalist, Creekview High School 2009
- Golden Apple Teacher, Polaris Evening School 2008

Doug Johnson

Blog: Blue Skunk Blog
URL: http://doug-johnson.squarespace.com/
Website: Doug Johnson's website
Website: http://dougjohnson.squarespace.com/
Twitter: @BlueSkunkBlog
Books and Publications:

- *The Indispensable Librarian: Surviving (and Thriving) in School Libraries in the Information Age, second edition.* Libraries Unlimited/ABC-CLIO, 2013.
- *The Classroom Teachers Survival Guide to Technology.* New York: Jossey-Bass, 2012.
- *School Libraries Head for the Edge.* Linworth/ABC-CLIO, 2009.
- *Machines Are the Easy Part; People Are the Hard Part: Observations about Making Technology Work in Schools.* Minnesota: Blue Skunk Press, 2004.
- *Teaching Right from Wrong in the Digital Age.* Linworth/ABC-CLIO, 2003.

About the Blog: Following the Blue Skunk Blog is something I've been doing since 2004, and I now follow Johnson on Twitter as well to make sure I don't miss a post. The technology, library, and media ideas and information that Johnson post are always refreshingly honest and original. Both personal and professional topics and views pepper his blog, and a couple of especially memorable posts include "Why Robots Make the Best Teachers" (August 6, 2012) and "Ten Top Reasons for Games in Libraries" (August 2, 2007). I find the Blue Skunk Blog to be a practical and common-sense approach to often overly complicated issues and times.

Gwyneth Jones

Blog: The Daring Librarian
URL: http://www.daringlibrarian.com
E-mail: gwynethanne@gmail.com
Twitter: @gwynethjones
Slideshare: http://www.slideshare.net/gwynethjones
Linkedin: http://www.linkedin.com/in/gwynethj
YouTube: http://www.youtube.com/gwynethanne
Flicker: http://www.flickr.com/photos/info_grrl
Pinterest: http://pinterest.com/gwynethjones/
Sqworl: http://sqworl.com/u.php?user=2228

About the Blog: This is one of the most visually appealing blogs and websites you'll find and use. It's no surprise that Jones's background includes advertising, marketing, and public relations. Jones's most current focus is on transliteracy, mash-up production, graphic design, mobile media, cutting edge librarians and fighting for our students.

Awards:

• Teacher Librarian Magazine, Visionary Leader 2012
• MSET Outstanding Technology Leader of the Year 2012
• Library Journal's Movers and Shakers 2011

R. David Lankes

Blog: Virtual Dave . . . Real Blog
URL: http://quartz.syr.edu/blog/
E-mail: rdlankes@iis.syr.edu
Twitter: https://twitter.com/rdlankes

Books and Publications

- *The Atlas of New Librarianship*. Cambridge, Ma: MIT Press, 2011.
- *Reference Renaissance: Current and Future Trends*. Radford, M., and Lankes, R. David (eds.). New York: Neal-Schuman Publishers, 2010.
- Lankes, R. David. *New Concepts in Digital Reference*. San Rafael, CA: Morgan-Claypool, 2009.
- *Virtual Reference Service: From Competencies to Assessment*. Lankes, R. David, Westbrook, L., Nicholson, S., Radford, M., Silverstein, J. (eds.). New York: Neal-Schuman Publishers, 2007.

About the Blog: Lankes is a professor and dean's scholar for the New Librarianship at Syracuse University's School of Information Studies and the director of the Information Institute of Syracuse (IIS), and his posts are so entertaining that one forgets that the source is scholarly and academic. Among news items, and recommended books and articles, Lankes's personal and professional thoughts and ideas urge librarians and the library profession to be all that we can be. His August 1, 2012, post that appears in Chapter 2 of this book implores librarians to stop fighting against Google, and all the other changes that have been said to threaten our well-being, but to be proud and vocal about what makes us invaluable to our communities. You don't want to miss this blog, his books, or his point of view.

Awards: *The Atlas of New Librarianship* won the 2012 ABC-CLIO/Greenwood Award for the Best Book in Library Literature.

Jennifer LeGarde

Blog: Adventures of a Library Girl
URL: http://www.librarygirl.net/
Blog: Level Up Book Club
URL: levelupbc.blogspot.com/
Twitter: @jenniferlagarde

Awards:

- Library Journal's Movers and Shakers 2012
- Salem Press's Best School Library Blog 2012
- Carnegie Corporation of New York/New York Times American Library Association I Love My Librarian 2011
- Edublog, Nominated Best Librarian/Library Blog 2011

About this Blog: Adventures of a Library Girl freely shares advocacy, literacy, technology, and lifelong learning resources and tips. LeGarde is a school librarian who puts her students first, and through her blog and Tweets, she provides examples and tools for engaging students to help them learn better.

LeGarde is one to watch—although in the field for only a handful of years, she has more energy, ideas, and passion than most.

Bobbi Newman

Blog: Librarian By Day
URL: http://librarianbyday.net
Twitter: @librarianbyday
Facebook: http://www.facebook.com/TheRealLibrarianbyDay
Linkedin: http://www.linkedin.com/in/bobbinewman
ALA Connect: http://connect.ala.org/user/35335
Pinterest: http://pinterest.com/librarianbyday/

About the Blog: Newman's blog reflects her multiple library-related interests and includes posts, discussions, and links to information within her categories of Libraries and Transliteracy, Libraries Day in the Life, This Is What a Librarian Looks Like, Training and Workshop, and Resource Site.

Bobbi Newman, Tom Ipri, Brian Hulsey, Gretchen Caserotti, Anthony Molaro, Lane Wilkinson

Blog: Libraries and Transliteracy
URL: http://librariesandtransliteracy.wordpress.com/
Facebook: http://www.facEbook.com/librariesandtransliteracy
Google Group: https://groups.google.com/forum/?fromgroups#!forum/librariesandtransliteracy
RSS: http://librariesandtransliteracy.wordpress.com/feed/
YouTube Video: http://www.youtube.com/watch?v=sk4Cw8vrDuM

About the Blog: This blog gets down to its transliteracy business quickly. Visually, it's all about the posts. The most recent post appears front and center on the homepage, and the large timeline of posts is easy to peruse. The helpful section and link "Beginners Guide to Transliteracy" provides the history, explanations, and articles to further your knowledge of transliteracy. In addition, a Reading List link takes you to either a short or a complete list of articles.

Awards:

• Salem Press, Best General Blog 2010
• Edublog, Best New Nomination 2010
• Edublog, Best Group Nomination 2010

Sue Polanka

Blog: No Shelf Required
URL: http://www.libraries.wright.edu/noshelfrequired/
Twitter: @spolanka

Books and Publications:

- *No Shelf Required 2*. Chicago: ALA Editions, 2012.
- *No Shelf Required*. Chicago: ALA Editions, 2010.
- *E-Reference Context and Discoverability in Libraries: Issues and Concepts.* Hershey, PA: IGI Global, 2011.
- *The No Shelf Required Guide to Ebook Publishing*, ALA Publishing (single issue magazine), 2011.
- "An Ebook Primer," *Library Journal*, April 15, 2012.
- "A Guide to Buying Ebooks." November/December, 2011, 30.
- *Advances in Library and Information Science Newsletter* 1, no. 1 (2011).
- "E-Factor: How E-books Are Making an Impact in Libraries," *Advances in Library and Information Science Newsletter* 1 no. 1 (2011).
- "Improving Library Services with Ebooks," *Information Outlook* 15, no. 5 (July/August 2011).

Additional columns and publications are listed on the No Shelf Required Blog.

Awards:

- Salem Press Great Academic Blog 2012
- Library Journal's Movers and Shakers 2012.

About the Blog: Although Polanka lives in the academic world, her blog is a must-follow for any type of library and librarian. Polanka brings the most up-to-date announcements, news, and issues from the eBook industry to her followers. There is so much information shared, and available, about eBooks that the best method is to have it pushed to you through her feeds and Twitter, one post at a time. Not sure how to market the eBooks in your library? A category for marketing is dedicated to providing information, discussion points, and upcoming events that focus on drawing patrons and users to available Ebooks. Not sure how to select titles and formats for your users? There is a Collection Development category for that. Other categories include School Libraries, Public Libraries, Print on Demand, Reference Publishing, and Mobile Devices. Just about any question or discussion about eBooks for which you are searching will be found through No Shelf Required.

Kathy Schrock

Title: Kathy Schrock's Guide to Everything
URL: http://schrockguide.net
Kathy Schrock's Home Page: http://kathyschrock.net
Kathy Schrock's Kaffeeklatsch: http://blog.kathyschrock.net
Twitter: @kathyschrock

Books and Publications (2007–2012):

- "Reading. 'Riting. 'Rithematic. Real life." *Library Media Connection*, M/J 2012.
- "Connecting your Classroom to the Future." *eGenio.com*, April 2012.
- "Infographics as a Creative Assessment." *eGenio.com*, March 2012.
- "R.I.P.: Respect for Intellectual Property." *eGenio.com*, January 2012.
- "A Dose of Twitter for Every Day of the Year." *eGenio.com*, January 2012.
- "Equipping Teachers to Infuse Technology." *District Administrator*, January 2012.
- "Authentic Learning for Students." *eGenio.com*. December 2011.
- "Manage and Maintain Your PLN." *NEAmb.com*, November 2011.
- "Must-have Tech Skills for Teachers." *eGenio.com*, November 2011.
- "Concept Mapping in the Classroom." *eGenio.com*, October 2011.
- "Literacy in the Digital Age." *eGenio.com*, September 2011.
- "Top Teacher Tech for 2011." *NEAmb.com*, August 2011.
- "Technology to Watch." *THE Journal*, January 2011.
- "Kathy Schrock's Top 12 Free Edtech Tools." *teachhub.com*, April 2010.
- "Synchronous Tools for Schools." *NEAmb.com*, December 2009.
- "Create Your Own Personal Learning Network." *NEAmb.com*, December 2009.
- "Top Teacher Tech: What's Hot for the New School Year." *NEAmb.com*, August 2009.
- "Second Life: Interactive Professional Development." *Hotchalk.com*, May 2008.
- "Second Life: Lighthouse Learning Island." *Hotchalk.com*, May 2008.
- "Nailing Digital Jelly to a Virtual Tree." *Learning & Leading with Technology*. December 2007.
- "Critical Evaluation in the Collaborative Era." *Technology and Learning*. November 2007.

Awards:

- Must Read Educational EdTech Blogs 2012
- Discovery Educator Network DEN Guru Award 2011
- Game Classroom's Top Educators, April 2010
- eCollegeFinder's top 50 Education Innovators 2010
- Edublog, Award Winner: First runner-up for Best Individual Blog 2009
- Bella Online Distance Learning Site of the Month 2008
- MassCUE Making it Happen Award 2007

About the Blog: Schrock's website is exactly what she says it is: a guide to everything. The technology resources offered through this site include an almost endless variety of topics such as apps, assessments and rubrics, creating your Professional Learning Network PLN, day in the life of an iPad, information literacy, QR codes, Twitter, and much more. School librarians as well as classroom teachers will find high-value tools to enrich their students' learning experiences. Confused about how to use Twitter as an educational tool? Check out Schrock's "Twitter" section titled, "Cure what Ails You: A Dose of Twitter for Every Day" for many more tips, links, and resources about using Twitter than you can imagine.

Joyce Valenza

Blog: School Library Journal's The Never Ending Search
URL: http://blog.schoollibraryjournal.com/neverendingsearch/
Twitter: @joycevalenza

Awards:

- Edublog, Lifetime Achievement 2011
- Edublog, Best Librarian/Library Blog 2011

About This Blog: By following Valenza in her blog and tweets, you will be introduced to the very newest emerging media tools and trends. The Never Ending Search keeps its finger on the pulse of the library media world, and you can relax and trust that the information you receive from Valenza is reliable and trustworthy. If Valenza recommends a new curation or collaboration tool, feel comfortable pursuing and sharing it with your community. She's been at this gig a long time, and her superhero cape is just a little brighter and shinier than the rest. She is a must to follow.

NETWORKING AND PROFESSIONAL DEVELOPMENT ARE POWERFUL

Multiply your learning potential by following the best of the profession.

AASL Advocacy Tip of the Day

URL: http://advocacytipoftheday.wordpress.com/

About the Resource: Receive the tip of the day by e-mail or by following it on Wordpress.com. You can read and use the advocacy tips, and you can submit your own tips for other readers to use. Tips include methods to shout your successes and to provide information to parents, administration, your entire community, and legislators. It's an easy and beneficial tool that is pushed to your inbox.

Discover Your Favorite Power Tools

ALA Connect

URL: http://connect.ala.org/

About the Resource: The ALA Connect website is a space where ALA members can meet and work together. Working Groups, Divisions, Communities, Round Tables, Sections, By Categories, and New Groups divide the social media space into smaller sections. Working tools provided by the website include polls, online docs, files, events, pictures, chats, and discussions. You can choose to browse topics or join in discussions in the open groups.

ASCD SmartBrief

URL: https://www.smartbrief.com/ascd/

About the Resource: The ASCD SmartBrief is a twice-weekly e-mail newsletter that provides education-related tips, technology news and projects, quotes, toolkits, news, webinar and professional development announcements, and a jobs hotline. Subscribe and peruse for subjects of interest right from your e-mail inbox. A quick yet broad scan of top education news and trends is pushed to your e-mail inbox.

NAMLE: National Association for Media Literacy Education

URL: http://namle.net/publications/core-principles/

About the Website: NAMLE began in 1997 as PME: Partnership for Media Education (PME) and is a membership-driven organization that offers members access to media literacy resources, discounts, and networking. NAMLE publishes the *Journal of Media Literacy Education*.

NCLE SmartBrief

URL: https://www.smartbrief.com/news/NCLE

About the Resource: The National Center for Literacy Education (NCLE) provides a twice-weekly newsletter for all issues connected to the teaching, learning, and advocacy of literacy. This newsletter is pushed to you through e-mail, and you can submit your own story or tips to share with others. Beginning in September 2012, the free e-mail newsletter became available as an optional feature of membership with the American Association of School Librarians (AASL) through collaboration with the National Center for Literacy Education (NCLE).

Library as Incubator Project

URL: http://www.libraryasincubatorproject.org
Twitter: @IArtLibraries
Pinterest: http://pinterest.com/iartlibraries/music-incubators/

About the Website: This website is the collaboration of Laura Damon-Moore, Erinn Batykefer, and Christina Endres, three very wise librarians. Library as Incubator Project exists to promote relationships and partnerships among libraries and other cultural and community institutions, primarily art museums and artists, by providing resources and physical space. Recent collaborations involve makerspaces located in libraries for all sorts of creating and making projects.

TRAILS

URL: http://www.trails-9.org/
Affiliation: Kent State

About the Website: Founded in 2004 and initially funded by grant money, this free resource allows teachers and librarians to assess the knowledge of students concerning information literacy and research skills. The assessment involves multiple-choice questions targeting a variety of information literacy skills based on third-, sixth, ninth, and twelfth-grade standards. I've used this resource to compare pretest and postinstruction knowledge in order to determine the effectiveness of specific instructional methods and information. This is a useful resource that changes and improves regularly, and the founders of the TRAILS tool also have a college preparation module to use with older students.

TRADITIONAL RESOURCES ARE NEW AGAIN

The following resources are traditional sources that are familiar to most librarians but that also provide additional information through social media or online features. Even after reading these traditional print sources cover to cover, you'll find new and fresh ideas through the online source.

Knowledge Quest

About the Resource: Journal of the American Association of School Librarians

URL: http://www.ala.org/aasl/knowledge-quest
Twitter: @AASL

Online Features:

• *Knowledge Quest* poll
• Calendar of Upcoming News and Articles in *Knowledge Quest*

- Podcasts of guest editors talking about their issues of *Knowledge Quest*
- 30 seconds Thought Leadership: current and past questions and responses by leaders in the school library field
- Webinars
- SLR: School Library Research related to *Knowledge Quest* themes and topics.

Additional Resources: Other AASL resources that relate to *Knowledge Quest* themes and topics.

Library of Congress (LOC) Professional Development for Teachers and School Librarians

URL: http://www.loc.gov/teachers/professionaldevelopment/
Twitter: @Librarycongress
Facebook: http://www.facebook.com/libraryofcongress
YouTube: http://www.youtube.com/libraryofcongress
Flickr: http://www.flickr.com/photos/library_of_congress/

About the Resource: Educational materials, primary sources, and news and events are offered through the LOC Professional Development site. In addition, the teacher institute, in-house training at the LOC, and videoconferencing are highlighted along with self-directed opportunities for professional development.

Library Journal

About the Resource: *Library Journal* has been one of the most respected professional publications for more than a century, and this online version offers what readers have come to expect, along with other features available only online.

URL: http://lj.libraryjournal.com/

Online Features:

- Webcasts
- Blogs
- Event News and Spotlights
- Latest Stories
- Opinion
- Technology
- Book Reviews
- Academic Libraries
- *Library Journal* in Print Archives
- Job Zone

Twitter: @LibraryJournal
Facebook: http://www.facebook.com/pages/Library-Journal/11249119181
Flickr: http://www.flickr.com/photos/libraryjournal/
RSS: http://www.flickr.com/photos/libraryjournal/

SLJ.com

URL: http://www.schoollibraryjournal.com/
RSS: http://www.slj.com/feed/

Online Features:

- Blogs
- Print Issue Archive
- Articles
- Webcasts
- Newsletters
- Book Reviews
- Technology Tools, Methods, and Philosophies
- Event News
- Job Zone

About the Resource: The online version of the print journal, *School Library Journal* (SLJ) includes the same print articles and news items, but also offers special online features that include breaking news and more.

Twitter: @sljournal
Facebook: http://www.facebook.com/SchoolLibraryJournal
Pinterest: http://pinterest.com/sljournal/
Tumblr: http://schoollibraryjournal.tumblr.com/
Vimeo: http://vimeo.com/user3904395
Flickr: http://www.flickr.com/photos/schoollibraryjournal/
E-mail: info@mediasourceinc.com
RSS: http://www.slj.com/feed/

Tech and Learning

URL: http://www.techlearning.com

About the Resource: This is the online version of the print journal *Tech and Learning*, which provides educators with invaluable news and information about integrating technology into schools and curriculum.

Online Features:

- Blogs
- Best Practices
- Contests
- Webinars
- Tech Forums
- Video
- Resources
- Magazine
- Product Reviews
- Tips
- Buyer's Guide

Twitter: @techlearning
Facebook: http://www.facebook.com/TechLearningMagazine

YALSA's Teen Book Finder by American Library Association

URL: http://www.ala.org/yalsa/products/teenbookfinder

About the Resource: This is an app to help teens, educators, librarians, and parents find YA literature published in the past three years. The app was developed for the iPhone and iPod Touch, so the screen is small on the iPad. However, users will not care when they discover all the features that the app provides. For example, users can share titles on Facebook or Twitter, find desired items in nearby libraries, and build a personal list of favorite titles. An Android app is being developed and should be available in late 2013

Selected Bibliography

American Library Association's (ALA) Association of American School Librarians (AASL). "Committees, Editorial Boards, and Task Forces." September 2012. http://www.ala.org/aasl/aboutaasl/aaslgovernance/ aaslcommittees/committees

Damon-Moore, Laura. "Mission of Library as Incubator Project." Library as Incubator. August, 23, 2012. http://www.libraryasincubatorproject.org/ ?page_id=9

Google. 2012. "MakeBeliefComix." The Literacy Project: Innovative Projects. July 5, 2012. http://www.makebeliefscomix.com/

Gorman, Michael. "Flipping the Classroom . . . a Goldmine." 21st Century Educational Technology and Learning. July 30, 2012. http://21century edtech.wordpress.com/2012/07/18/flipping-the-classroom-a-goldmine -of-research-and-resources-to-keep-you-on-your-feet/

Gutierrez, Peter. 2012. "Pop Culture Press Releases: Use These Real-World Models as Prompts to Writing and Critical Thinking." *School Library Journal*: *Connect the Pop: At the Intersection of Pop Culture, Transliteracy, and Critical Thinking*. August 10, 2012. http://blogs.slj.com/connect-the -pop/2012/08/comics/pop-culture-press-releases-use-these-real-world -models-as-prompts-to-writing-and-critical-thinking/

Hamilton, Buffy. 2012. "Makerspaces, Participatory Learning, and Libraries." *Unquiet Librarian*. June 28, 2012. http://theunquietlibrarian.wordpress .com/2012/06/28/makerspaces-participatory-learning-and-libraries/

Hive13. "About Hive." August 7, 2012. http://www.hive13.org/

Inanimate Alice. "About the Project." July 31, 2012. http://www.inanimatealice .com

Johnson, Doug. "BYOD and the Library." Blue Skunk Blog. March 10, 2012.
    http://doug-johnson.squarespace.com/blue-skunk-blog/2012/3/10/byod-and
    -the-library.html

Lankes, R. David. "Beyond the Bullet Points: It Is Time to Stop Trying to Save
    Libraries." *Virtual Dave . . . Real Blog*. August 7, 2012. http://quartz.syr
    .edu/blog/?p=1697

Polanka, Sue. "ALA Program Summary: E-Elephant in the Room." *No Shelf
    Required*. July 21, 2012. http://www.libraries.wright.edu/noshelfrequired

Robin, Bernard. "The Educational Uses of Digital Storytelling." August 6,
    2012. http://digitalstorytelling.coe.uh.edu

Sheketoff. 2012. "Don't Wait to Be Empowered." AASL Advocacy Tip #317.
    July 21, 2012. http://advocacytipoftheday.wordpress.com/2012/07/20/
    advocacy-tip-317/

StoryCorps. 2012. "Day of Remembering." StoryCorps. August 20, 2012.
    http://nationaldayoflistening.org

Index